THE
MURDER
of
CHRIS KYLE
AN AMERICAN HERO

Inside the Donald R. Jones Justice Center courtroom where the trial for the murders of Chris Kyle and Chad Littlefield was held.

ROBERT F. BLEVINS

ARCHWAY
PUBLISHING

Copyright © 2017 Robert F. Blevins.

All rights reserved. No part of this book may be used or reproduced by any means, graphic, electronic, or mechanical, including photocopying, recording, taping or by any information storage retrieval system without the written permission of the author except in the case of brief quotations embodied in critical articles and reviews.

Archway Publishing books may be ordered through booksellers or by contacting:

Archway Publishing
1663 Liberty Drive
Bloomington, IN 47403
www.archwaypublishing.com
1 (888) 242-5904

Because of the dynamic nature of the Internet, any web addresses or links contained in this book may have changed since publication and may no longer be valid. The views expressed in this work are solely those of the author and do not necessarily reflect the views of the publisher, and the publisher hereby disclaims any responsibility for them.

Any people depicted in stock imagery provided by Thinkstock are models, and such images are being used for illustrative purposes only.
Certain stock imagery © Thinkstock.

ISBN: 978-1-4808-4334-9 (sc)
ISBN: 978-1-4808-4336-3 (hc)
ISBN: 978-1-4808-4335-6 (e)

Library of Congress Control Number: 2017901342

Print information available on the last page.

Archway Publishing rev. date: 03/17/2017

Contents

Introduction vii

Day 1: Wednesday, February 11, 2015 1
Day 2: Thursday, February 12, 2015 13
Day 3: Friday, February 13, 2015 21
Day 4: Monday, February 16, 2015 29
Day 5: Tuesday, February 17, 2013 37
Day 6: Wednesday, February 18, 2015 49
Day 7: Thursday, February 19, 2015 57
Day 8: February 20, 2015 67
Day 9: Monday, February 23, 2015 83
Day 10: Tuesday, February 24, 2015 85

Closing Arguments 95
The Verdict 103
Characters of the Trial 107
Definitions 113
About the Author 117

Introduction

I followed the media of the murder of the American hero Chris Kyle and his friend Chad Littlefield. The influence of a higher being kept telling me over and over to attend the trial for this senseless murder. After learning when and where the trial would be, my journey to honor these two fallen men began.

The question is, why me? Why I was called to do this can only be explained by considering that I have been a retail business owner and baseball coach most of my life. As I look back, I know the coaching was a God-given talent that I was called on to share by the same influence that came to me about this trial. Because of my past experiences in retail and being with the public in general, I gained a talent for insight into the varying character traits of many people and developed the stamina and patience to follow through with the tasks put before me, whether it be closing the sale or developing a young athlete to his or her full potential. Perhaps this is why I was called on to share the details of the trial that will be presented in the days to come.

Why am I so drawn to travel to this trial? Why am I determined to honor Chris Kyle? During my pondering, I find myself reminiscing of the stories I heard as a child from my mother. She was the daughter of Syrian immigrants who passed into this country through Ellis Island. Her sister, the eldest child of ten, made the journey alone to reunite with her parents in America. Zekia, like many others, came to America with only a sign around her neck to identify who she was. The next nine children of Monsuer and Shahena Massad were born on American soil. In modern times, the unrest in the Middle East caused the family to consider themselves Lebanese as that country was more favorable at the time, so we are accustomed to saying our ancestors come from Lebanon or Syria. The Massad family began in America as merchants. Some still carry on that tradition, but others became doctors and other important professionals.

Serving the United States of America was among those professions. General Ernest L. "Iron Mike" Massad was my mother's first cousin and highly regarded in the family. Another of her cousins, Victor Farris, was in the US Air Force Intelligence for many years. I remember the story of my uncle Woodrow Massad, the youngest of the ten, who was lost at sea for three days. When found, he was so swollen his life preserver had to be cut away from his body. My father was a diesel mechanic on a ship in WWII. His younger brother was killed in the invasion of France.

These are all stories that have made me proud to be an American. Service to our country goes deep in my family. Perhaps I am honoring my ancestors as well as Chris Kyle. They are all American heroes.

Day 1: Wednesday, February 11, 2015

On Wednesday, February 11, 2015, in the Erath County city of Stephenville, Texas, Eddie Ray Routh, former US Marine, stands trial for the February 2, 2013, capital murders of Navy SEAL Chris Kyle and Chad Littlefield. The jury consists of ten women and two men, with two alternates. The first day of the trial starts at 9:00 a.m. in the Donald R. Jones Justice Center. Judge Jason Cason presides. District Attorney Allen Nash and Jane Starnes from the Office of the Texas Attorney General are there to prove that Eddie Ray Routh knew what he was doing and knew it was wrong.

The defense attorneys for Eddie Routh are Tim Moore, R. Shay Isham, and J. Warren St. John, and they are here to prove he is insane. R. Shay Isham is a tall, dark-haired man of average weight and complexion. Tim Moore has a reddish complexion and is heavier but not fat, of average height, with light-colored, curly hair.

Eddie walks in the courtroom dressed in a dark suit, a blue shirt, and a gold-and-blue tie. He is big and stout and appears strong. He is at least one hundred pounds heavier than he was in the pictures shown on TV when the murders were committed. His dark hair is cut short and spiky, like some sort of hybrid crewcut. With the extra weight, his face and cheeks are full, and he sways his head back and forth as he walks. His heavy black-framed glasses fit his character well, with his cold black eyes piercing right through the lenses. This is the man who shot Chris Kyle, the American hero who earned twelve medals for his service to our country, and also killed Chris's friend Chad Littlefield. These were cold-blooded, senseless, and tragic murders.

This is the defendant who should be found guilty but could be found not guilty or insane.

The prosecution is about to make their opening statement. Everything is quiet, and tension is thick as District Attorney Allen Nash takes long strides walking to address the jury and court. He is a tall man with light-colored hair and looks to be fortyish. He is well dressed, wearing a suit and tie, as all the attorneys are. The jury is hanging on every word. As he speaks, DA Allen Nash never loses eye contact with the jurors and the defense.

DA Nash states that Eddie Ray Routh shot Chad Littlefield seven times with a 9-mm handgun, four times in the back, once in the hand, once in the head, and once in the top of the head. He then shot Chris Kyle six times. There were five shots to the back and one in the head with a .45-caliber handgun. Then Eddie Ray ran, got into Chris Kyle's black, diesel, four-wheel-drive pickup truck and drove away, heading toward Oklahoma City on I-35. Eddie had smoked marijuana and drunk whiskey the morning of the shooting.

District Attorney Allen Nash concludes by stating, "Mental illness does not keep a person from knowing right from wrong. He is a troubled man."

While the prosecution's tone is positive, secure, and confident, the defense's statement seems doubtful. I notice a bit of a cracking voice as the defense attorney representing Eddie Routh, Tim Moore, begins. He seems determined to push ahead no matter the consequences.

Attorney Moore says, "He has psychosis and wasn't in his right mind. He is a high school graduate of Lancaster, Texas. He graduated in 2006, served in Iraq, and was honorably discharged from the marines. He is known for having a drinking problem. He was admitted to the VA hospital in Dallas and diagnosed with psychosis in July of 2011. When released, he was prescribed antipsychotic medication but was readmitted to the VA hospital in August of 2011. Eddie was diagnosed as suicidal. He lived with his mom and dad in September of 2012. The police stopped him walking down the road on January 19, 2013. The defense claims Eddie Routh had a psychotic episode and went back to the hospital, where he was given more antipsychotic medication and released on January 25. Eddie went back to his parents' house. On February 1, 2013, the night before the murder, Eddie was hearing and seeing things. On February 2, 2013, the morning of the killings, he drank whiskey and smoked marijuana. Chris Kyle picked Eddie up. Chris was driving, and Chad Littlefield was on the passenger side in the front seat. Chris Kyle texted Chad Littlefield, 'This dude is straight up nuts. Watch my six.'

"Eddie was going to take Chad's and Chris's souls before they took his," says attorney Moore.

The first witness is Taya Kyle, the widow of the American hero, who has been left without the love of her life to raise their two children alone. She is a beautiful, well-dressed, and elegant-looking woman who has had her heart and her world ripped from her and her family because of the senseless acts of Eddie Routh. Taya is confident but nervous and manages to present herself with a composed manner, but still you hear her voice break when answering some of the questions. You can tell she wants to be a good witness, and determination to secure justice for her husband's and his friend's murders is the driving force that gets her through her testimony. She takes the stand and answers the attorney's questions about the life of her murdered husband. The prosecuting attorney helps her along to nail points about the honesty and integrity of her husband and our American hero's character—Taya's husband, but also the man who fought out of dignity and love for the United States of America and who also belongs in the hearts of all American patriots.

Taya says she is forty years old and from Portland, Oregon. She tells the district attorney that Chris's birthday was April 8, 1974. Chris and Taya met in San Diego in 1999, where he was in the process of completing BUD, basic underwater demolition training, for the navy.

Chris Kyle was an alumnus of Tarleton State University in Stephenville, Texas. Mr. Kyle got out of the navy in 2009. "He was known as a fast draw," says Taya. He was also known as one of the most decorated US Navy SEAL snipers and as the Devil of Ramadi. He had 160 kills that were witnessed and paper-worked and served four tours in Iraq. He served six eight-month deployments. Chris had two Silver Stars, six Bronze Stars, one valor navy, a marine corps commendation medal, and two navy and marine achievement medals.

When I watched the movie *American Sniper*, it left a great impression on me, especially during the portrayal of Chris showing empathy for the enemy when he reverted back to his life in the United States. He wondered what he would do if it was his child being looked down upon through the scope of a sniper. But the child he spotted in his scope picked up a grenade launcher. This American hero was in Iraq to protect the American troops and our country, which meant he was to take out anything or anyone that was a threat.

The family moved to Texas because "it's the best place to live," says Taya Kyle on the witness stand. Chris trained in self-defense with pistols and rifles and worked at Craft Interventional, cofounded by Chris in 2009. It is a security, defense, and combat weapons training company for military, police, corporate, and civilian clients. Taya Kyle owns 85 percent of the company. The company logo is a skull and crosshair. The crosshair is on the right eye to honor Ryan Job, who was critically wounded with a gunshot to the eye.

Chris set up a long-distance shooting range at Rough Creek Lodge, which had a restaurant, petting zoo, pond, and flowers.

Chris and Taya had a boy and a girl. She becomes visibly upset at this time and starts crying but manages to go on to say, "Chris worked to help people recover."

Rough Creek has fishing, hunting, and shooting. Chris came and went as he wished. He had night sweats and was 33 percent disabled but looked great. Chris met Chad Littlefield on a soccer field. Their girls are the same age. Before the book *American Sniper* came out, both had humble, simple lives and were hard workers. Chad and Chris usually worked out together, starting at five in the morning in

Chris's garage. Marcus Luttrell, a Navy SEAL who received the Navy Cross and Purple Heart, believed that one day outside was a much better place to heal and to become more serious and talk around the campfire at night.

Taya Kyle says, "Eddie's mother asked Chris to meet with her son to see if he could help him. She gave Chris a note with a number on it."

Chris had never met Eddie, and neither had she. Chris owned a 350 Ford, and it wasn't kept real clean. He basically lived in it. On February 2, 2013, she was taking their daughter to Build-A-Bear Workshop. Chris, Chad, and Eddie left to go shoot. Chris had a replica of a Colt 45 with him. The last time Taya Kyle saw Chris, they told each other, "I love you." At 2:00, Chris called Taya and was very short. She texted Chris that she was getting worried but never received a response.

A police officer pulled up to the house. Officer Mark Tradley told Taya, "Chris has been hurt," and took her to a friend's house. Officer Tradley asked if she had seen Chris's truck, and she told him she hadn't. Taya called her mother and told her something was wrong.

Taya Kyle's testimony is truthful, and she has been struggling to hold up for all the love she holds for this man and all that he is to her and her family, who have been dragged through hell because of the violent tragedy. She pushes on no matter what, fighting off tears and anguish. She is all that is left for her two children and must know what a difference Chris would have made as the father of their family. What a great loss to their family and humanity!

Mrs. Starnes, from the Office of the Texas Attorney General and representing the prosecution, asks Taya about how Chris treated gun safety. Taya says, "It was always a big concern, and the barrel of the gun always had to be up or down, even if it was a toy."

During the cross-examination, Taya is asked if she has been deer hunting with Chris, and she says she has. The defense attorney wants to know if Chris ever drank while he was hunting or when he was just shooting and if he drank a lot.

Taya says, "Maybe a beer, but he never mixed alcohol and guns."

Chad's mother is the next witness. She grew up in Harlingen, Texas. Chad was born in Dallas on February 11, 1977, and graduated from De Soto, Texas. Chad grew up in Dallas. He was a logistics manager at a water plant. Leanne was his wife and is a middle school assistant principal in Midlothian, Texas. They have a daughter named Morgan. Chad also worked for an electric wheelchair company. Chris and Chad met on a soccer field where both of their daughters played soccer. Chad and Chris worked out together and lived seventeen miles apart. Both called often to check on their parents. Mrs. Littlefield says, "Chad didn't talk much, but he was a good listener. He had a DHL license, since he wasn't military."

"The last time I saw Chad was February 1; he talked about the Bible," Mrs. Littlefield says. "Chad needed to brush up on his Bible studies because he didn't want his daughter, Morgan, to know more about the Bible than he did. When he left, he hugged me and then walked off and came back to hug me again. I found it unusual."

Mrs. Littlefield was called at about 9:00 p.m. and was told Chad had been in an accident. It was later in the night when she found out he was dead. Jane Starnes asks if Chad wore cologne.

Mrs. Littlefield says, "He like good cologne, not cheap cologne either. He was the type of guy that would take a bath before he went swimming." His hobbies were deer hunting and fishing. His dad was a football coach. Chad was a conservative, well-groomed person. Chad told his mother that it quit being about him when his daughter was born. He didn't do drugs and was usually the designated driver.

Frank Alvarez is the next witness to take the stand. He states, "I have been the manager of Rough Creek Lodge since January 1998. Rough Creek Lodge is on Highway 67 and covers one thousand acres. It has a restaurant, fishing, hunting, and horseback riding." Mr. Alvarez continues that the lodge also provides trap shooting, and a long-range shooting facility was established in May 2010 by Chris Kyle. He established the location, distance, and structure for the lodge and brought organized groups to the range. The lodge has Mallard Lake, kid bike ranching, Ping-Pong, tomahawk throwing, archery, and paintball. The lodge has house leasing and a processing room to clean birds. The lodge is in three counties and has dog kennels with an average stay of fifty days.

Mr. Alvarez says on February 2, 2013, he received a call that Chris Kyle was at the lodge. He says that he met with Chris, and Chris told him he was going to go shooting. Mr. Alvarez told him to be sure to raise the bravo flag. Mr. Alvarez got a call from the lodge dispatcher saying that he needed to go to the range. Arriving at the range, Justin Largo met him and told him Chris was down and bleeding. Mr. Alvarez then saw three men working on Chris. The three EMT responders, David, Bobby, and Matt, were working on Chris with a defibrillator and doing compressions. Chris, Chad, and Eddie Routh had been at the shooting range for about forty-five minutes.

The trial breaks for lunch, and I go to my car to get a legal yellow pad to replace the three-by-five memo book that is all I found in my suit pocket after being told to take my bag back to my car this morning. This being my first day to have ever attended a capital murder trial, I had quite a learning experience this morning and will not make the same mistakes again. At 7:00 a.m. there was already a very long line waiting to enter the court. There were people from Austin, Texas, and Washington. I didn't ask if it was DC or state, but I couldn't understand a word he said. A reporter from Austin, Texas, translated for me. California folks were everywhere. I had a bag with me with water, a tape recorder, paper, pens, and my cell phone. I saw a sign that said, "No electronics, phones, or bags beyond this point." I thought I would just set it down and leave it in the building outside the courtroom and go ahead and walk in. But oh, no! Security told me to take the bag to my car and get back in line. I rushed my belongings to my car and hurried back to get in my place in line as quickly as I could. I feared I would not make it back before the court filled to capacity. I was the next-to-the-last person to be allowed in the courtroom. I made it just in the nick of time! Tomorrow I will bring legal pads and pencil only. I don't want any more trouble. As long as I get in line between 6:00 and 6:30 a.m., I can feel confident that I will have a place in the courtroom. Security opens the doors at 8:00 a.m. and allow only five people to enter at a time. Court starts at 9:00. Family usually show up at 7:45 and are escorted into the court first, then the media people, and us common folks last. There are 115 seats in total in the courtroom.

After lunch break, court resumes at 1:00 p.m. sharp, so I get in line all over again and go through the metal detectors.

Beginning the afternoon session, the defense's objection to the use of photo thirty-five is denied by Judge Jason Cason. There were a lot of photos of the crime scene. Photo thirty-five was of the murder scene, with one body on the wooden platform and the other on the dirt.

Mr. Alvarez continues on the stand and is cross-examined by the defense.

The defense asks Mr. Alvarez the approximate time it took to get to the location and how many people worked on Saturday. He answers, "There were over one hundred that day. It took five to six minutes to get to the location." The defense asks about the brass on the ground, whether the brass had been picked up or not. Mr. Alvarez replies, "It is picked up after every use. There was a lot of money lying on the ground."

The defense makes a comment that the defendant mentioned there were a lot of brass on the ground. The defense is done with the cross-examination of Mr. Alvarez and sits down.

Next the prosecution calls Justin Largo to the stand. Justin is married, has a son and daughter, and is a part-time wildlife guide. Justin is about five foot eleven, thirty something, and has a rough, outdoorsy look about him. He teaches safety in archery and paintball and conducts scavenger hunts. He has been working at Rough

Creek Lodge for twenty-three months. Justin says he went to work on Saturday, February 2, 2013, at 9:00 a.m. He didn't know Chris personally but he recognized his truck. He was trying to help one of the boys he taught meet Chris Kyle. He wanted to speak to Chris, but he saw the red bravo flag was up, signaling that fire was going on. All shooting activities are guided. At 4:40 to 4:50 Justin saw the flag was still up, so he put on ear protection, but no shooting was going on. Approaching the shooting range, he saw an assortment of rifles and pistols as he drove up in a mule all-terrain vehicle. He saw one body on the ground and one on the platform. He immediately called 911.

Justin tells the jury, "Chris was on the ground, and Chad was on the platform. Chris was facedown but was rolled over when the paramedics arrived so they could work on him. When the paramedics arrived, I told them I thought Chris still had a pulse, but the paramedics said they were both dead."

The defense calls Bobby, an off-duty eight-year fire department lieutenant who showed up at the scene. He spent eighteen months as an army medic. He heard the call at 17:30 to 17:40 and knew the nearest trauma center was in Fort Worth. Bobby responded, thinking he might be of some help. He says of when he arrived, "I saw blood in Chris's hair and the abdominal area." He also testifies, "Medic two and a helicopter were in route to transfer Chris and Chad."

Prosecution next calls Matt Green, the driver of the ambulance, to the stand. He also saw two unresponsive men that day. He testifies, "Chad was not breathing, no heartbeat, and his skin was a pale, ash color. I saw a shot to Chad's head and arm and brain matter next to his head on the platform."

Officer Martin is next to testify for the prosecution. He states that he was assisting a traffic accident with the state police when he heard a call come in between 5:00 and 5:15 p.m. that two parties had been shot. He was the nearest officer to the scene. He traveled through another county to get to the long-range shooting facility. Upon arriving, Officer Martin took control of the scene. He asked everyone to step back except the medics working on Chad and Chris. He searched Chad's pockets for identification and found none. He then searched Chris and found a wallet in his front right pocket.

Officer Martin says, "Employees of the lodge were in shock and said it made the hair on the back of their neck stand up. They had never seen such violence." Officer Martin tells the prosecution he felt that he had preserved the scene of the crime.

In cross-examination, the defense asks the witness what road he took to get to the scene of the crime. Officer Martin says, "Highway 199."

Officer Martin must have known the area very well. He seems very confident that he took the best route to arrive at the scene as soon as possible.

The next witness prosecution calls is Mrs. Harris. She says she has worked three and a half years for the police department as a dispatcher on the graveyard shift from 6:00 p.m. to 6:00 a.m. Mrs. Harris says, "I took the 911 call from Laura Blevins, Eddie Routh's sister. Laura reported that she was 'afraid for her life.' Eddie had told her he had kill two men at a shooting range and he was in a Ford 350 black or dark blue pickup. They were en route to the police station to make a formal statement. Laura said, 'Eddie has been known to drink in the past.'"

Next witness for the prosecution is Chet Kelly. Chet says he works for the water department and was friends with the Littlefield family. Chet's wife, Vanessa, was at a twirling competition in Oklahoma City when the murders occurred. Vanessa called the Littlefields between 7:00 and 8:00 p.m. to check on Chad because they had been hearing some things.

This is all for today, and court adjourns. After looking for a place to eat, I am going back to my room. I don't have a clue what I am doing or what is going on with the trial. But I do know I am getting up tomorrow morning and going back to the trial with my yellow legal pad and pen.

When I finally get to my room, I am emotionally drained.

Reflecting on today's testimonies, I wonder what I have put upon myself. Mr. Nobody from Oklahoma here is trying to absorb the heart-rending details of this trial. I know there is more to come, like the description of witness Matt Green of the murder scene and the pictures of the scenes that have been shown so far. I can't get them out of my head. My heart and soul ache for the families of the victims.

Day 2: Thursday, February 12, 2015

Eddie Routh struts into the courtroom. He seems to think he is really something with all eyes on him, as if he were a celebrated superstar, pretentiously dressed up in a dark suit and gold print tie.

Several Texas Highway Patrol officers in uniform with freshly pressed white shirts and silver badges are present, plus about twelve more roaming around outside the courtroom. Four Texas Rangers stand at the doors going out of the courtroom. More rangers with a mix of highway patrol officers are scattered around the corners of the room and throughout the seating area. One mean-looking guard with a shaved head who is not in uniform stays with Routh at all times, including escorting him in and out of the courtroom. The officers periodically walk up and down the aisles, looking to see what is in everybody's lap.

Texas is not about to get another black eye over this trial by losing control and letting this turn into a Lee Harvey Oswald/Jack Ruby repeat. I was in the eighth grade when that happened. I remember it was bad enough for Texans that President Kennedy was shot and killed in their state, and then there was the ordeal of Jack Ruby killing Oswald before the state had the chance to prosecute him.

Tensions are high. I can see the stress on everybody's face, looks of anger, bewilderment, and anxiety. You better not even pick your nose. It is best to sit down, stay in the same seat, and not move until break. When the judge comes in, the bailiff says, "all rise," and when the judge sits down so does everyone else. The jury comes in, and we all repeat the process. You don't talk. You listen. If you leave, you can't return until break. These guys are dead serious. All the officers wear boots, hats, guns, and handcuffs. The rangers wear special cowboy boots with Ranger imprinted onto the leather. You name it, they've got it, and they are not smiling. One stocky ranger gets my attention. The name on his shirt says Oliver.

The prosecution calls Texas Ranger Matt to the stand. Ranger Matt says he was a Texas Highway Patrolman who then made ranger. He does crime scene photos, low-light photos, fingerprints, trace evidence, and hazardous material. Ranger Matt received a phone call to go to a crime scene Saturday, February 2, 2013. He goes on to say that rangers have the ability to call all hands on deck. He arrived at 10:00 p.m. and found two males shot multiple times. He used a laser to map out the area. He found a lot of brass at the scene. He mapped out the shell casings with the photos. Ranger Matt used a camera that takes a 360-degree angle picture with twenty-two megapixels. He then puts the film on a disc and checks the photos for any red flags, which he can zoom in on.

Ranger Matt continues, "Weapons were found on Chad and Chris. Pistols were holstered and loaded. Chris and Chad were taken by surprise." Ranger Matt found all kinds of guns in no apparent order lined up on the shot board, which is the designated area for guns to be placed when they are not in use. There was a black handgun positioned on top of the railing lying right above Chad's head. There was a western-looking single-action gun resting beside Chris's hand with six spent rounds still in it. Ranger Matt refers to it as a "dry gun," meaning all shots had been fired. There were 9 mm casings around Chad's arm and a casing by Chris's right ear.

Judge Cashon calls for a recess at this time. We take a break at 10:40 and have only ten to fifteen minutes to get back to our seats. I count again, and there are twelve highway patrol officers, four rangers, and six assorted police officers. If you go outside, you have to go through the metal detectors again, but it takes too long and makes it almost impossible to get back to the courtroom in time, so I don't go outside. I am living and breathing courtroom and trial because I don't want to miss a second of it.

I am observing Mrs. Kyle. She is wearing a black and white dress and a large watch on her left wrist. She is wearing her diamond ring on her right hand. She's a very pretty lady with dark, straight hair. I see anguish, anger, and an anxious nervousness about her. The nervousness I believe comes from her determination to do her part to make sure justice is served for the murder of her husband and his friend. She will do everything in her power to make that happen. Again, my heart goes out to her and the families.

Sitting in my seat, I am grateful it is well padded and has oak elbow rests. Chris's parents sit two rows up. The families occupy almost half the courtroom. I am in the last row of seats in this section. There are some seats behind me, but I am actually in the last half row of the section where the family sits.

The break is over, and the next witness for the prosecution called is Lancaster, Texas, Police Officer Salazar. He has nine years and four months' service, spent nineteen years in the marines, and was a marine ranger instructor. He testifies that he helped stop Eddie Ray Routh. Officer Salazar put stop sticks under the back tires of Chris's Ford pickup. Eddie made a run for it, and Salazar said Officer Grimes was first to reach the Ford when it was finally disabled at I-35 North off of Highway 20. Officer Salazar testifies that at that time they only knew the driver was a suspect in a murder case.

There's a break at noon. The bailiff shouts, "All rise." The jury leaves first, then the family, and then the news reporters and us common folks. We have one hour to be back from lunch. If I leave the building, I will have to go through the detectors and stand in line at the entrance to the courtroom. Some people can't make the morning session but come to the afternoon session, so there is a good chance if I come back and find myself last in line, I won't get back into the trial for the second half of the day. There are only so many seats available in the courtroom. So, I just hang around inside. Again, I don't leave for fear of missing a word.

After lunch break, Officer Salazar is still on the stand. He is recounting details of the chase of Chris Kyle's pickup that Eddie Routh was driving. Also, the prosecution is playing the video from Officer Salazar's dash cam. Salazar was using two cameras during the chase. He had a shoulder-mounted camera and a vehicle camera in operation.

He describes chasing the pickup. "That pickup ran good. Eddie was trying to outrun us. They went seven blocks or more at his speed of about a hundred miles per hour. Then he took a side access road to I-35 North."

About then as it shows in the video, the truck was t-boned by a patrol vehicle. I can see metal flying in the video. The patrol vehicle bounced off the truck, and Eddie Routh kept going. Finally, the chase began to slow down until the truck became inoperative. The video shows Eddie getting out of the truck with his hands up and lying down on the dark pavement. Six officers immediately rushed to him and handcuffed him. By now there were about fifteen to twenty officers on the scene. Officer Salazar was alone in a Crown Vic, Unit #1455. The chase had been through pedestrian walkways and Oakland Park. The court watched all of this on a screen video taken from the dash camera from Office Salvador's vehicle.

Officer Salazar is a DRA, or drug recognition expert. He talks about marijuana dipped in PCP or formaldehyde or Purple Heart. He states, "Eddie could have been on one of these, but no one knows except Eddie."

The prosecution then turns witness Officer Salazar over to the defense for cross-examination.

The defense attorney stands only to reference a comment Eddie made at the scene of the apprehension. The defendant said, "Pigs, that smell, the pigs. They were going to get my soul, so I got their souls."

The prosecution calls Officer Mike Logan to the stand. He

has twenty years and four months of service and is lieutenant over criminal investigation. Officer Logan says he was called to 221 Sixth Street in Lancaster, Texas. This was the residence of Eddie Routh. He had been informed that Eddie Routh's sister contacted police and sent them looking for a Ford pickup. Eddie was from Lancaster and had a dog. Officer Logan knew Eddie and didn't think he would leave town without his dog. Officer Logan arrived at 221 Sixth Street and found Eddie in the truck. He tried to talk Eddie out of the truck. The truck had tinted windows, so Officer Logan couldn't see what he was doing. A phone rang inside the truck, and Eddie started talking to someone. Another officer wearing a body cam ran down the street toward Eddie. He got to the truck and also made an attempt to talk Eddie into getting out. This was Officer Salazar, and he talked Eddie into rolling the window down. Eddie and Officer Logan were neighbors. They carried on a half-hour conversation in front of the residence, with Eddie in the truck and Officer Logan on the street trying to get him out of the truck. All of this was being recorded by Officer Salazar's body cam. All of us in the courtroom were watching this on the screen.

Eddie was saying, "Everybody wants to barbeque my ass." In the video, you can see Eddie in the pickup with the window down about five inches on the driver's side. He can be heard saying, "I want to see my mom and daddy. I don't know what it's all about. I can't trust the world. I want to go see my parents in Abilene." The officers continued to try to talk him out of the truck. All of a sudden, Eddie started the truck and sped off. Four police cars were immediately in pursuit. Officer Salvador was the fifth car to join the chase. He had both his body cam and car cam recording.

At one time when I was young and working the wheat harvest in Northwest Oklahoma and Kansas, I had to operate a bus that had a broken speedometer, so I had to learn to count the skip lines marked on the highway to judge the speed I was driving. The count of one thousand one to three skip lines meant sixty-five miles per hour. Watching the video recording of Officer Salvador's dash cam, I counted those skip lines. I believe Officer Salvador got up to about 120 miles per hour before he managed to maneuver his vehicle into first place in front of the other four patrol vehicles. This positioned his cameras so they were able to record the whole thing, including the chase and the arrest.

Dr. Barnard is next to be called by the prosecution to provide information about the autopsies he performed on February 3, 2013, on Chad Littlefield and Chris Kyle. It was case number 229 at Southwest Forensics in Dallas County, Texas.

Dr. Barnard is standing with a pointer describing diagrams achieved from the autopsy of the corpses. He explains, "Chris Scott Kyle had multiple gunshot wounds. He was fully clothed, six foot one, two hundred sixteen pounds. He had six gunshot wounds, a tattoo of a cross, and a tattoo of a frog skeleton. He showed positive for venlafaxine, an antidepressant, in his blood. One bullet entered his cheek and came out the back of his neck. The second bullet, in the back of his shoulder, had no exit wound and went through an artery into the lung. Bullets three and four went into the upper right arm and went through the humerus. One bullet ended up in the armpit, and the other exited the body. Five went into the abdomen and exited the backside of the abdomen, going through both kidneys. Six was an abdomen entrance and went through the liver and colon. The bullets are listed as bullets, not in order that they were fired."

Mrs. Kyle looks up, fighting off tears. She lowers her head and begins to cry, sucks it up, and then raises her head again, trying to hold back the tears as long as she can. Emotion just flows from her for the love of her lost husband. The pictures of the scene are gruesome and sad.

Dr. Barnard continues. "Chad Littlefield was six feet tall, two hundred thirty pounds and had earplugs in both ears. He had a multicolored tattoo of Jesus and the name Morgan tattooed on his left arm. Seven bullets had entered his body. One on top of his head that exited out the bottom of his skull. Bullet two entered to the left of his nose and exited the back of his shoulder. Three entered the back of the head and exited the neck, behind the right ear. Four entered the upper right shoulder and exited slightly lower. Five entered the lower right back and exited the right chest. Six entered the middle of the back, went through the spine, and exited the front of the chest on the right side, straight across. Seven entered the back side of the hand and exited the front side of the hand."

That concludes Dr. Barnard's testimony. He steps down, and that concludes day two.

The bailiff says, "All rise" in a loud voice. The jury moves out of the courtroom through a door next to where they sit, then the family, and then the news reporters and observers leave together.

This day was emotional and leaves me feeling sick and physically exhausted. You hear of and watch crimes on TV and don't pay a lot of attention to them. But in the courtroom with the pictures and drawings shown of each specific wound and exit, it all becomes too real. It is like watching a horror movie—one that stays to haunt you forever. I think that it has to be a special type of person who makes a career of investigating murders. The average psyche is not equipped to cope with this gore and brutality day after day.

Day 3: Friday, February 13, 2015

It's a cold morning, and as usual, I'm standing in line at around seven o'clock. Today I meet Bryan, a longtime friend of Chris Kyle's who went to school and graduated with him. Bryan tells me that Chris was a really easygoing guy. I asked Bryan what Chris liked to do growing up.

He said, "Chris liked to hunt and fish. He played football, and he was a forward in basketball."

I say to Bryan, "Why was the killing so vicious?"

He says, "Eddie was just mean about it."

Bryan drives an hour just to get in line like all of us, just to see the trial. I tell Bryan that he should be with the family. The next time we enter the courtroom, I notice that he is sitting with the family. I am glad I said something about that.

If you don't get in line early, you don't get in the courtroom. We watch while the family is escorted by police. Car lights flash, and after parking they enter the south side of the justice center about fifteen minutes until eight. The door opens at about eight o'clock. Only five people are allowed through a security check at a time and are put through metal detectors. Security is very tight, and everything is looked at closely. I've yet to get a seat any closer than third row from the back.

I notice Taya Kyle is holding on strong. She is wearing a black and white dress with black and white pumps. She always presents amazingly well.

Eddie Routh struts in as usual. His hair is short, and today he is dressed in a power suit. He seems a confident man in this dark suit, white shirt, and red tie. I feel him look at me. At least I think he did, but I am sure he is just looking at everyone. If it were me, I would have my head down and not seem proud at all.

Today there is a new set of Texas Rangers, young, tall, tough, nice looking, clean-shaven men. One ranger has white handles on his semiautomatic pistol. I later find out this is Ranger Holland. General Patton had ivory handles and once told a reporter, "Only a pimp from a cheap New Orleans whore house would carry a pearl-handled pistol." That's what I ask Ranger Holland, if they were pearl. He just says, "No, they're ivory." The rangers of Texas are a class act and the real deal.

The prosecution calls Sergeant Stewart to the stand for introduction. He has been in law enforcement eighteen years. Sergeant Stewart testifies about various pieces of evidence that were retrieved from the crime scene and Chris Kyle's pickup. Sergeant Stewart was responsible for labeling and storing each piece of evidence from the crime scene.

Next to testify for the prosecution is Ranger David Armstrong out of Dallas. He has movie star good looks and has been a Texas Ranger for three years with twelve previous years in law enforcement as a Texas Highway Patrolman. He explains, "Only those with the top test scores are selected for rangers, and then they have to go to ranger school."

He says that he got involved in the murder case when Eddie and the black Ford pickup had entered into Dallas County. He took pictures of the I-35 scene. Mr. Armstrong identifies Eddie in the courtroom by describing what he is wearing and where he is setting.

He says, "I found a loaded handgun in the driver side door and a bolt-action rifle between the console and front seat of the pickup. The guns went to evidence."

"Myself and four other rangers entered the Routh residence on 220 West Sixth Street in Lancaster, Texas. We started a counterclockwise search through the eleven-hundred-square-foot, three-bedroom house.

This is the Routh family home. Eddie slept in the guest bedroom in the northeast corner of the house. In this room, we found drug paraphernalia, a glass pipe, and a tin can with a grinder in it, a bong, rolling papers, a bottle of Crown whiskey, prescription medication, and a note on the wall with Chris Kyle's phone number on it. The whiskey bottle was found on the table and almost empty with a glass next to it. There was also an assortment of ammunition found, including a box of fifty full-metal-jacket nine mm shells."

The defense decides to cross-examine. Up to this point in the trial, the defense hasn't said much to the witness. They want to see Ranger Armstrong's case notes. He doesn't have them but says he can get them. The defense asks what time Ranger Armstrong arrived on the scene.

Ranger Armstrong says, "Eight forty-five, and I didn't talk to Eddie." The defense asks if anyone smelled alcohol or marijuana on Eddie. Armstrong says, "No. Eddie was handcuffed in the backseat of a Lancaster police car, and I had waited at the police station until the judge signed the warrant to search the house where Eddie stayed. I met with four other rangers before beginning the search. Eddie's mom also lived there, but Eddie's father had moved."

The district attorney returns to the stand and asks Ranger Armstrong if they found a dog bed. He says, "No."

"Did you find a dog?"

Again, the answer is "No."

The defense rises again and asks Ranger Armstrong, "Did you smell marijuana in the house. Is that why you got the search warrant?"

The ranger says, "I said that I had not been to the house yet to smell the marijuana." The spectators in the courtroom laugh under their breath. The defense sits down, and the judge calls for a short recess.

I think it was a dumbass question from the defense team and out of sequence. I am still thinking about it and mumbling to myself in the bathroom during recess. I even voice my thoughts to the person in the stall next to me. The man makes no comment. I figure out why later when I am called into a meeting with the bailiff. It turns out the man in the bathroom is there for the defendant. He complained to the bailiff. The bailiff warned me that if he heard of me voicing my opinion about the trial to anyone again I would be banned from attending. I was sincerely apologetic to the bailiff. In addition, I sure would have also been very apologetic to the six-foot-five or so brick wall of a man in the bathroom if he would have confronted me. I watch what I say from now on, even under my breath to myself. No more thinking out loud about the trial allowed for me!

After recess, the defense calls James Watkins to the stand to testify on behalf of Eddie. There is an older woman who shows up today for the trial with two young children. They take a seat on the defense side. I think the children are Eddie's, and the woman is his grandmother. James Watkins is Eddie Routh's uncle. James is from Alvarado, Texas. He goes on to say that Alvarado is thirty miles south of Dallas Highway 67 and I-35.

He says, "Eddie grew up in Lancaster, Texas, and they are God-fearing people." Eddie's mom worked with special education children. Eddie worked on small arms in the marines and later repaired small arms for a company he worked for. James says, "Eddie spent four years as a marine in Iraq. He came back from Iraq and went to Haiti on a humanitarian effort, and that Haiti trip affected him more than Iraq."

He goes on to say that Eddie had trouble finding a job. Eddie was frustrated that he had lost the love of his life. James says that Eddie lived with him for almost a year. He slept on the couch. After meeting Jen Weed, he moved back to his mother's house. His father, Raymond, who is a machinist, worked on cattle equipment. James says that Eddie had never had his own house. He had a half-ton pickup and then sold it and bought a red and white VW beetle. The last time James saw Eddie was Christmas of 2012. James got a call to go and see Eddie from Jodi, who is Eddie's mom and James's sister. He showed up at 220 West Sixth Street in Lancaster, Texas, at about 8:00 in the morning. Eddie told James he and Jen Weed were having trouble with their relationship. They had talked about the Bible and how he didn't like living with his mother. They smoked some marijuana. James is forty-five, and he had been smoking since he was a teenager. James says the marijuana they smoked that morning was "good weed." They smoked a couple of bowls. He says it was normal to drink whiskey and smoke marijuana in the morning.

James says between 10:00 and 12:00 on February 2, 2013, he heard someone walking on gravel toward the house. It was Chris Kyle, who picked Eddie up and then left. Eddie had mentioned he was going to the gun range about one o'clock. James says he locked his sister's house and went home. James says Eddie has mental and physical problems, is unemployed, and has anxiety and depression. James went home, got in his recliner, and took a nap. This is James's story of the day of the murders.

Later he was woken up by Eddie saying, "I am driving a dead man's truck." James thought Eddie was talking about himself.

James says that Eddie at the time got mad and offended easily. He was frustrated with his cabinet-making job and felt underappreciated. He had a fight with Jen Weed on February 2, 2013. The prosecution asks James if he was on probation. James doesn't look like he wants to answer but replies yes. Mrs. Starnes asks why. He tells her it's for assault on an ambulance employee. James had previously talked to Ranger Briley four times and lied to him about smoking marijuana. Mrs. Starnes sits down.

The defense asks James to confirm that Eddie's mother is his sister. The defense also asks about Eddie's discharge from the military. James says Eddie joined the marines after high school and had an honorable discharge.

The defense continues. Ranger Briley had asked James if the marijuana he and Eddie had smoked the morning of February 2, 2013, was laced with anything. James told him it wasn't; it was just normal weed.

James is asked, "What do you do when you smoke?"

James says, "Just sit around and enjoy it." He doesn't recall drinking whiskey on the morning of the murders.

James is a big man with a thick chest and shaved head. He wears black-rimmed glasses and has a deep voice, and his face looks swollen, with a short black beard.

The defense continues asking James about when Eddie was picked up. James says he and Eddie were on the front porch when Chris picked Eddie up. James says he was high for about three hours, and then Eddie popped in at James's house and said, "Look at my gun and truck." Both belonged to Chris Kyle.

The district attorney asks James if Laura Blevins is Eddie's sister and if she smoked marijuana with Eddie. He replies, "Yes." He goes on to say that Eddie had been smoking marijuana regularly since he was seventeen years old.

The district attorney then calls James Jeffress to the stand. He works for the Texas Department of Public Safety as a forensic scientist specializing in ballistics. Mr. Jeffress explains that bullets leaving the barrel of a gun leave microscopic marks on the bullet because the barrel of a gun is a harder metal than the bullet. The hammer of the gun also leaves marks on the ejected shell casing. The guns from the firing range were test fired into a five-hundred-gallon water tank so a bullet could be analyzed about where marks are made. After examination of the bullets, Mr. Jeffress says they received a black Ford pickup and photos of all sides of the truck, including the glove box, tool box, and bed. A Remington 700 3006 Springfield rifle and a Sig Sauer double action handgun with an anchor imprinted on the left side of the handle were found in the driver's side door. Mr. Jeffress testifies he received nine 9 mm casings, eight .45 automatic casings, two .223 casings, eleven Remington .38 special casings, six .45 colt casings, three .308 Winchester casings, a .38 Cimarron revolver, and a .45 colt Cimarron casing. There were no long gun shell casings, and all casings were matched. The gun in the door was a fourteen-inch gun with a one-inch chamber. Mr. Jeffress demonstrates how long it took to put fourteen bullets in the 45 and the 9-mm handgun. He also demonstrates how long it took to unload and reload the colt 45 replica single-action gun made by Cimarron Arms Company. Mr. Jeffress says that out of the ten guns tested, only four matched with casings from the scene. No shell casings from the long guns matched.

Gene Cole, ex-sheriff and current patrol deputy for the Erath County sheriff's Office, is called to the stand by the prosecution. Officer Cole has one year of service with Erath County. He came in contact with Eddie and testifies he heard Eddie say, "I shot them because they wouldn't talk to me. I feel bad about shooting them, but they wouldn't talk to me. I sat in the back of the truck, and they wouldn't talk to me."

Day 4: Monday, February 16, 2015

It is sleeting and extremely cold today. The prosecution calls Sergeant Phillips, who is a detox expert, to the stand. He has thirteen years of experience in law enforcement. He picked Eddie up from Lancaster, Texas, at around 3:00 a.m. on February 3, 2013. Captain Upshaw instructed Sergeant Phillips to take Eddie's clothes from him in the processing room. Eddie was wearing cowboy boots that had brown tops and tan bottoms. Sergeant Phillips says, "He was under the influence and a candidate for detox."

The prosecution calls Ranger Ron Pettigrew to the stand. He spent seven years as a Texas Highway Patrolman and five years as a Texas Ranger. He testifies that he was responsible for securing Chris Kyle's truck to the Garland, Texas, laboratory. He found two phones in the truck, and one was Chris's. He also found a billfold in the console.

The defense rises to cross-examine Ranger Pettigrew, who assisted in serving the search warrant and searching Eddie Routh's house. Ranger Pettigrew responds that it was an undercover agent who was familiar with buying illegal drugs, knew about making narcotics, and knew the language. The defense asks what the term *wet* means. Ranger Pettigrew replies that it means marijuana can be laced with formaldehyde, PCP or purple heart, ecstasy, and other types of drugs.

Next on the stand the prosecution calls Ranger Mike Gunter. He is a five-year ranger from Cleveland, Texas. He covers Johnson and Somerville Counties. He was contacted by Ranger Briley to take photos of the crime scene. He transported the photos to the Garland, Texas, crime lab.

Banging his gavel, the judge orders the lunch recess right on the dot of noon. I don't go anywhere. I just get back in line inside the Donald R. Jones Justice center. You never know how many people are going to show up for the afternoon session. Today's crowd produces a line inside and outside the justice center. There are lots of inquisitive people, lawyers, law enforcement, law students, etc. All kinds come to see who did this and why it happened. Jay Novacek, Dallas Cowboy tight end with three Super Bowl wins, is somewhat of a regular. He is a friend of Chris Kyle's family; you can tell by how they talk to each other.

The family leaves the courtroom first. As usual I am sitting two rows behind the victims' families. Today Chris Kyle's dad walks over to me as he passes. He has noticed my yellow note pad and asks me in an offensive tone, "Are you a reporter?"

I tell him, "No, I am here to honor your son."

He later apologizes for snapping at me. I accept his apology, and he smiles and walks away with Chris's mother. I am sure he approached me with intentions of asking me to leave. I am glad he realized the sincerity in my words to honor his son.

Jeff Shaffer is the next witness called by the prosecution. He is a former secret service senior special agent and now specializes in electronic forensic science and cybersecurity. He attends two or three schools annually and has examined approximately two thousand phones and mobile devices. He examines material for authentication using a RF shield room to save the integrity of the data. Shaffer talks about how a number is assigned to every phone. He received Chris Kyle's and Chad Littlefield's phones. He checked the MR files, voice mail, and the call log.

Eddie left a voice mail to Chris saying, "Looking forward to talking to you," another saying "Give me a shout," a third saying, "Sad day when it rains. Missed you," and a fourth saying, "Give me a call back." There were two missed calls from Chris to Eddie. This showed that Chris Kyle and Eddie Routh were communicating back and forth before the murder. Mr. Shaffer also examined the call from James Watson's phone to Jen Weed verifying all information from the phone extraction.

The prosecution calls Texas Ranger Danny Briley up to the stand. He has seven years of experience as a Texas Ranger and ten as a Highway Patrol Officer. He spent six years in the Seminole Sherriff's office in Erath County. Ranger Briley goes on to explain that he got his crime scene education at the Tennessee Bureau of Investigation. He has the ability to reconstruct crime scenes and preserve evidence. He arrived between 5:45 and 6:00 p.m. at the Rough Creek Lodge crime scene. He was looking to see what happened. He found shell casings, struggling gunshot wounds, and gun splatter.

"It was an absolute internal kill," says Ranger Briley. "It was very violent, and there was an exceedingly uncommon amount of shots fired."

An excellent marksman trained in combat skills is the only one who would have the skill level to kill Chris Kyle. Rangers called in a team to process the crime and identify who the perpetrator could be. They had found out the whereabouts of Eddie Routh through Laura Blevins around 7:50 and were going after him with every resource they had, including a SWAT team on standby. Lancaster officers learned Routh was at his residence. They tried to contain him there and wanted to arrest Eddie at his home. Ranger Briley was there to attempt an interview with Eddie. He left the crime scene because of the chase. He drove approximately 105 miles to the residence from the crime scene.

He explains how to do an interview, saying, "Be soft and compassionate, don't lie to the suspect, and ask simple questions that can lead to details of the crime. Then pay attention to what they are saying and if it's truthful, pretending, denying culpability, answering questions quick, recognizing questions but not answering, or rearranging questions. It's necessary to build a rapport and try to get a good portion of the truth."

When Ranger Briley was put in the interrogation room with Eddie Routh, he read him his rights and started out by saying, "I know you had a tough day." Ranger Briley asked Eddie if he had done any drugs that day. Then he asked what happened. Eddie responded in a philosophically posed manner and started comparing pig shit to horse shit. Ranger Briley wanted to know if Eddie knew what he was doing and if he knew what he did was wrong. Eddie Routh confessed to killing Chad and Chris and stated that what he had done was wrong.

Ranger Briley states, "Eddie said it was wrong to kill them and he was sorry he did it."

The DA turns on the video showing Eddie in a chair with his hands cuffed behind his back. His head is lying on the table, looking to his left. After a while he lifts his head up and leans back in the chair. You can tell by watching that the cuffs were starting to bother him. You can feel and see the eeriness surrounding Eddie as he sat alone in that room with the realization of what he had done. Ranger Briley had left the room. He came back in and sat down.

Eddie started talking. He said, "It's sad the way it happened. Talking to Chris was like talking to the wolf. I could smell his shit."

Taya Kyle stands and leaves the courtroom during the video. Today she is wearing a dark purple dress with dark gray pumps with some sort of print in the shoe. She always looks good. She has streaked her hair slightly. I imagine she doesn't want to hear this crap from Eddie, and I don't blame her. A nobody, saying he could smell this hero's shit.

Ranger Briley continues in the video by asking Eddie about himself. Eddie explained he was born and raised in Lancaster, Texas, and graduated from there. After graduation, he joined the marines. He spent four years in the military but was never a member of a squadron. Eddie became a prison guard and worked on guns.

Eddie said, "Chris was protecting the school where my mother worked." He called Chris and Chad headhunters and said, "When I looked them in the eyes, they were going to get my soul."

Eddie said, "I saw my sister today. I told her, 'I had to kill a man today because I was going to get my head shot off.'" He told Ranger Briley he killed one with a Sig Sauer 9 mm pistol. "I was right up close to them. I didn't want to shoot them."

He said, "I shot Chad first. If I didn't take his soul, he was going to take mine. They were playing chess with my life." Pure adrenaline and some tobacco he says is all he was on and said he can't sleep at night. "I can't sleep in that world; it's about getting everybody healthy."

Ranger Briley asked "Do you know right from wrong?"

Eddie said, "After I killed them I knew what I had did was wrong. I should do more thinking than hurting people." Eddie was asked if he smoked pot that day and said he used it and, "That is the only thing that relaxes me. I am trying to fix what is wrong with the world. I am a common man and tired of missing out on my life because of this shit. Chad and Chris were telling me what was happening in my life, and they talked to me pretty shitty. They weren't nice to me." Eddie said, "Chad never shot at any of the targets. So I asked him, 'What are we here for, hunting for props?'"

Ranger Briley asked Eddie, "Where did you shoot Chris?"

Eddie paused and said, "I would like to see my mom one last time. I am sorry for what I've done. We can work this out. Is Mom and Dad in town? I want to see them. Can you get these cuffs off?"

Ranger Briley asked, "Did you shoot Chris with the 9 mm?"

Eddie said, "No, that be the other guy. They laid there till three o'clock or so."

I feel real nauseous right now, being here watching and hearing this testimony, visualizing what really happened to these two good men, sons, husbands, and fathers. Listening to Ranger Briley interrogating Eddie, a person can really get a feel for what happened that afternoon February 2, 2013. It was a violent and bloody murder.

I have never before sat through a capital murder trial. I am watching this skinny man on video being interrogated in a small room sitting at a table with two chairs and now seeing him in the courtroom in a suit and overweight. He doesn't even look like the same person. I can almost taste the horrendous murder. All those shots, thirteen in all, and being here is so violently real that I feel physically ill. I would bet that Eddie is not the same person who left the crime scene. He is sober now and taking regular medications.

The chain of events progresses to when Eddie is at his sister's house and he is asking her if she wants to see his guns. He tells Laura he is sorry for what he did. Ranger Briley brings into the courtroom Eddie's clothes, blue pullover with white horizontal-striped shirt, jeans, and cowboy boots that Eddie wore at the Glen Rose Range crime scene. Ranger Briley asks if the marijuana he smoked was dipped in formaldehyde because it goes up in smoke and can't be detected. Eddie said, "No." He was then asked if he knew the difference between right and wrong. He replied, "Yes."

In my opinion, these are two completely different personalities—the skinny Eddie who is paranoid and on drugs and the overweight Eddie clinically medicated and sober.

Eddie Routh showed no emotion, no smile, no tears, no frown, nothing, not a sign of feelings. Ranger Briley asked him why he ran from the police, and he gave no answer, and why he surrendered—also no answer.

Ranger Briley asked, "What are you going to tell your mother and sister?"

Eddie replied, "I'll tell them I love them." When asked, "Would you take it all back, what you did?" he gave no response. When he was asked, "Did you know there was blood on your boots?" Eddie replied, "Little bit."

There is a pause in the testimony. I put my head down to think. When he shot Chad Littlefield in the head at close range, there is a good chance Eddie actually saw the blood hit his boot. I believe Eddie envied Chris's military status, especially Chris the hero, the Devil of Ramadi. He was something, someone to look up to, and Eddie was nobody and he knew it. Chris and Chad were trying to help Eddie, but he felt like he was being put down and belittled.

Ranger Danny Briley is still on the stand. The video of his interrogation of Eddie Routh is over, and he is commenting on Eddie Routh's mind and where it was with a killing like this and how an intoxicated person has trouble with reality. He talks about how formaldehyde can't be tested. It is a gas. Eddie Routh's wallet held the military credentials of a marine, a TNT pay stub, and a hunting license.

The defense now cross-examines Ranger Briley and begins to set up a timeline of the day of the murders. "James Watson shows up at Eddie's house at about eight to nine a.m., right?"

Ranger Briley comments, "Yes," and goes on to say Chris's last call was at 12:30 p.m. and he left with Eddie at 1:07 p.m. The defense says that Eddie smoked marijuana about 12:30 p.m. The straight-up nuts text Chris sent Chad was at 2:30 p.m. Frank Alvarez's meeting was at 5:00 p.m. at Rough Creek Lodge. The employees found the bodies at about 5:00 p.m. Eddie went to his uncle, James Watson's, house at 5:00 p.m., and around 5:45 p.m. he went to his sister Laura Blevins's house. Laura called 911 at 6:50 p.m. Eddie was at Taco Bell in Red Oak, Texas, at 7:53 p.m. Eddie was in front of his house in Lancaster, Texas, with police at 8:30 p.m. Eddie Routh was arrested in the video between 11:00 and 11:15 p.m.

Ranger Briley comments on Eddie Routh words, "The war lords are not very happy with me today." Briley states, "As far as I am concerned, he was further indicting himself."

On further cross-examination, the defense says to Ranger Briley, "He illegally waived his rights."

I am thinking that the defense team doesn't have much and they are grasping at anything they can get their hands on. The excerpt from the statement given by Laura Blevins at the Lancaster police station repeating what her brother told her—"I have to take care of souls before they take care of mine"—exposes the truth about Eddie according to Ranger Briley. The defense talks about Eddie while Ranger Briley is on the stand, saying that Eddie had antigovernment issues.

"A lot of Eddie's conversations are nonsensical," the defense says. "He likes to say shocking things. He was angry at Chris and Chad. Things are not good in his life." The defense is trying to get some sympathy from the jury.

Tim Moore, one of the three attorneys for the defense, is talking. He is two steps from the jury box. He has his nose right there in the jury's faces. Mr. Moore makes a comment that Ranger Briley interviewed James Watson five or six times.

James had said, "Eddie said a person can defend himself when in apparent danger."

The DA stands up and fires right back, saying, "Was apparent danger present when he shot them in back? He shot them right up close. Chris and Chad didn't know he was going to shoot them. They were caught off guard."

The DA says, "I think Eddie thought his training was better. Remember the time and when he ran. He thought he could cover it up forever. Eddie knew Chris was a hero. Both were good men, and he shot them in the back. Chad was on the ground when he was shot in the top of his head. Eddie was proficient in the use of firearms. He knew that he shot Chad in the head, the face, and the back. He remembered how many times each were shot and said, 'I am sorry, I had to shoot them. I would be better if I could get these handcuffs off.' Chris and Chad's handguns were both holstered and loaded. Eddie Routh was never in threat of danger at the hands of the two murdered men."

The defense says, "So the ranger and the DA were comfortable with the decision to press charges against Eddie Routh."

This concludes testimony for day four.

Day 5: Tuesday, February 17, 2013

Journalist staff writer Tasha Tsiaperas of the *Dallas Morning News* asked if she could interview me about the trial. I didn't think I had time, but said maybe later. Sure enough, the perky little Greek reporter found me later. This time I took time to speak with her. She was very nice and sincerely interested in what I had to say. Tasha asked me how many times I had been present at the trial.

I told her, "Every time. I haven't missed a day and don't want to." She asked me why, and I said, "This is how I can honor Chris Kyle and what he did for this country."

I haven't said much about Judge Jason Cashon, but since I have gotten familiar with him by being at the trial every day, I have come to be entertained by his character. His personality type seems like he could have been a judge at any time in history. He makes statements like, "Who is riding this horse?" and no one disagrees that he is in control of the trial. He comes off as a stern, no-nonsense, and fair judge to me.

He just well could have been the hanging judge from Texas. I have no proof of that, but he certainly is a proud Texan. But to think of it, it seems everyone I meet from Texas is proud to be a Texan. My father, Gib Blevins Sr., grew up in Grapevine, Texas, and went to school with Clyde Barrow. When we visited Texas from Oklahoma, as soon as we passed the state line he would say, "Smell that air? We are in God's country. We are in Texas!"

Mrs. Kyle shows up today wearing black pants and a black top with gold shiny trim and black wedge heel pumps. She is truly a beautiful woman, and there is no doubt why Chris married her. She is strong and thin, and like my oldest son, some might say a lean, mean fighting machine. Mrs. Kyle wears dog tags every day. I am sure they belonged to Chris. She has a large watch on her left wrist and a beautiful diamond ring that she wears on her right hand. She bears up very well for what she has been through.

Today Eddie Ray Routh is wearing a dark suit, red tie, and blue shirt. He rolls in as usual.

The Texas Rangers will periodically walk down the aisles, looking between the seats to check what people have in their laps inside the courtroom. These guys really keep an eye on things, and as far as I am concerned, Texas Rangers and Texas Highway Patrol are doing a really good job securing this trial.

The defense and prosecution are in front of the judge discussing a mistrial! I hear this and think, *A mistrial! Surely not after all the preparation by the prosecution. And, what about that nagging feeling that drove me here?* The discussion about a mistrial was cultivated from a mistake when the lab included a glass vial with the items that were found in Eddie's bedroom. The vial from the lab had been mistakenly put in a tin can that was apparently Eddie's stash box. The vial with a clear liquid in it was not present at the home of the defendant. The testimony was presented by Ranger Armstrong. The judge instructs the jury to disregard the evidence because the vial didn't belong to the defendant.

Jennifer Rumple was put on the stand and questioned by DA Alan Nash about the glass vial. She has worked at the Garland Crime Lab for nine years and is an illegal substance tester. Rumple described three ways to test drugs. One is chemical color tests, but they vary on substances and block law enforcement from determining the substance. Two, the evidence is viewed under a microscope. Three, there is a color test on the THC taken from the plant. It is a different substance once burned and is no longer marijuana. She called the stash can a mail box. The vials were separated as evidence, and the jury was told to disregard the vial as evidence.

This is the defense team's attempt for a mistrial. It was not possible to prove that Eddie smoked pot laced with formaldehyde right before Chris picked him up because formaldehyde evaporates back to a gas. The defense had made this point. Expert witness Jennifer Rumple was in agreement that you cannot test for formaldehyde after it is smoked.

A mistrial is not granted.

The prosecution calls Amber Moss to the stand. She is a pretty girl with long black hair. She wears black glasses and a black coat. She is thirty-five years old and has worked for the Texas Department of Crime lab in Garland, Texas, for six years. Moss confidently explains that she is a DNA forensic scientist with a BAS in molecular biology, a branch of biology that deals with the molecular basis of biological activity. "This field overlaps with other areas of biology and chemistry, particularly genetics and biochemistry."[1] Moss analyzed the combination of DNA evidence Ranger Ron Pettigrew had. She explains that the analysis of DNA is our genetic blueprint, and cells viewed inside saliva vary from person to person. Genetic analyzers help analyze the DNA. They wear protective clothing and change gloves frequently to prevent cross-contamination. The blood spot on the right boot toe of Eddie Routh was Chad Littlefield's to the eighteenth quintillion. All blood spots found were Chris's or Chad's. There was no cross-contamination.

The defense rises to cross-examine Amber Moss. The attorney asks her if she has worked for six years and then rechecks her credentials.

Amber Moss tells the defense that duplication to the eighteen quintillionth can only happen with identical twins. Compare that to the earth's population of 7 billion. She performed DNA tests from the guns at the crime scene, particularly the revolver, and it was determined to be Chris's DNA.

---

[1] https://en.wikipedia.org/wiki/DNA_profiling

I can't hear the defense and what they are saying. They won't use their mics.

The defense sits down, and the DA resumes and asks about the DNA from the truck. Moss testifies that the DNA on the inside door handle was Chris's, Eddie's, and an unknown. The DNA from the steering wheel was Chris's and an unknown person's.

The witness is excused. As I watch Amber Moss make the long walk to exit the courtroom, for some reason it seems like it is taking forever. Every eye in the courtroom seems to be watching her. You could hear a pin drop.

Officer Salazar is called back to the stand by the DA to view video, especially concentrating at the end when Eddie Routh was arrested. The crowd around Eddie was distraught when he was getting in the police car and the door closed. You can see him in the backseat of the squad car where he was arrested on I-35 northbound after the high-speed chase. Eddie appears relaxed in the video from inside the police car. He leaned his head back, seeming to think, *What have I done?* He lies down in the squad car. You can hear him breathing. He sits up and asks someone outside, "How are you doing today, sir?" There is no answer. He lays his head back again after sitting up. The officer gets in and starts driving. Eddie says, "I don't know what's sane or not sane. I've been paranoid all day." I would have been paranoid too if I had just killed two men in cold blood.

The Eddie we see on trial in the courtroom today is not looking up as much. He just sits at the defense table and doodles with his head down. He did look up when the DA got disgusted and during the viewing of autopsy pictures, but not much anymore.

It is dead quiet in the car now. All you hear is the Crown Vic police car hitting bumps in the road, stopping, and accelerating while headed to the Lancaster, Texas, police station. Officer Salazar parks the car, and Eddie Routh is escorted into the police station.

Officer Salazar is an Iraq veteran. The DA is asking him if he is familiar with the drug trade in Iraq.

The trial adjourns. "All rise," says the bailiff. The jurors leave, then the family, then the rest of us.

Chris's father walks up to me for a second time. This time he asks if I am a veteran. I say, "No." I think I may be puzzling him just a bit. He smiles and walks off with his wife. The rest of us exit the courtroom. Chris's dad is a very proud and honest man. You can tell by looking at him and talking to him. He is trying to find closure; that is all he has left of Chris.

I feel a bit out of place, an outsider, around Chris Kyle's father. I personally have the memories of my ancestors and experiences of friends who have served. When I was eighteen, the Vietnam conflict was going strong. My draft number was very high, so I was not drafted. A lot of young men back then were afraid and hesitant to enlist. My friends who enlisted or were drafted came back mentally messed up. I will never forget Gary Nolan, a good friend and one of the members of my high school mile relay team. When Gary returned from Vietnam, he brought his Green Beret uniform to me and said, "I don't want to ever see this again." I stored the uniform, and we never spoke of it again. I would like to have a conversation with Mr. Kyle to let him know that I admire the work Chris was doing with veterans who come home damaged. He was a hero in battle and on the home front.

It is Tuesday afternoon on the fifth day of the trial.

I am observing Chad Littlefield's mother and father. Mrs. Littlefield is short in stature, has frosted hair, and looks like an intelligent and nice lady. She dresses well and handles herself well on the jury stand. Observing the trial with her is her husband, Chad's dad, who is a former policeman and coach. He is a big man with gray hair and a wide nose. He always has his arm on the back of the seat around his wife. The Littlefields are 50 percent of this trial but are somewhat shadowed by the more recognized Kyle family. This is understandable due to Chris's noted accomplishments. Nonetheless, the heart-rending tragedy affecting the two families is equal.

Captain Jason Upshaw is the next witness for the prosecution. He worked for the Tulsa Police Department in 1997 in narcotics. He explains that he is over the administrative records and staff of the jail where Eddie Routh was held. He explains the defendant had access to a TV and phone and was placed in a single cell. Officer Upshaw is asked if he could monitor phone calls. He states that he can monitor all phone calls and record them and that inmates are notified that calls can be monitored. The defense asks Officer Upshaw if he could hear both sides of the conversation, and he replies, "Yes."

The prosecution turns on a recorded conversation that took place on May 31, 2013, between Eddie Routh and reporter Nicholas Schmidle from *NY Magazine*. The defense immediately stands and objects to the self-incriminating and very damaging recording being played to the jury by the prosecution, but Judge Cashon overrules.

After the recording says, "One dollar and twenty-five cents and fifty cents for each additional minute," the reporter is heard asking questions to Eddie Routh about shooting Chris. "So Chris handed you a forty-five?"

Eddie said, "So I picked up a nine mm and shot a round and reloaded. The smell in the air smelled like shit. Took care of business, took off to see my uncle. Still had the nine mm with me. The targets were twenty-five and fifty feet. Shooting is not a spectator sport. You are supposed to shoot. Chris was shooting right beside me. Shot Chad first. Chris had just finished a magazine. Shot Chris second. Forty-five worked better."

Eddie told Nicholas Schmidle, "I told Laurie. I couldn't trust Chad and Chris. It smelled like sweet cologne in the truck. I was riding in the backseat. Went to my uncle's first, then to Laurie's house."

I am starting to figure out the plan that Eddie might have had during the events that led to him shooting Chad and Chris. Eddie would have needed Chad to be shooting so he would be distracted from him watching Chris's back. Somehow Chad was talked into shooting—maybe when Eddie said, "Shooting is not a spectator sport. You are supposed to shoot." I think as soon as Chad started shooting and Chris had emptied his gun, Eddie started firing at both of them—first at Chad, who was still shooting, and then Chris, who was holding an empty gun. This is my unprofessional opinion.

Jennifer Weed, Eddie's girlfriend, had tried to call Chris Kyle's phone that day when they were on the way to the shooting range.

The defense asks, "Had Eddie quit taking his medication?" Then they refer to a comment Eddie made while in jail: "Had to kill them before they killed me." The defense says, "He has been to two or three different psychiatrists. The jailer had been bringing medication to Eddie."

The district attorney replies, "He had medication on February 2, 2013, prescribed and re-prescribed to him. He has a calmer physical condition. His behavior has changed without illegal drugs."

The DA says, "Eddie had no fear of Chris and Chad."

The defense asks, "Has he been taking his medications prescribed?"

"Yes," replies Captain Upshaw. "His behavior has changed, and he gained one hundred pounds."

The defense jumps and says, "You have no idea whether he was taking the medication or not!"

We are now entering the defense portion of the trial. It is now the defense's turn to call their witnesses.

The jury is removed from the courtroom while the defense brings Greg Pruitt to the stand to explain how he locked up evidence from Rough Creek Lodge on February 2 and 3 of 2013. The guns that were selected for evidence, he explains, had stayed in the vault until today, February 16, 2015. Mr. Pruitt opens the sealed gun cases. The defense attorney is rubbing his right ear. I guess he thinks he has something. Eddie has his head up and is looking at the guns displayed in the courtroom. There are five guns that were received from the agent and that had been locked away. The defense declines to question the witness. The witness steps down, and the jury members return.

The defense calls Ranger Adcock. He explains that the evidence was spread out at the crime scene and other guns collected are not evidence. Eddie's head is up again, and he is looking interested in what is going on. Ranger Adcock is asked by the defense to identify a gun. He puts on his own red latex gloves from his pocket. The first gun identified is the AR 15 platform semiautomatic 7.62. He demonstrates how the magazine fits. The second gun he identifies is the AR 15 platform 223 caliber scoped for a thousand yards. The third gun, a .223, has the same platform with smaller projectile jacket. The fourth is a 7.62 rifle. On the buttstock, the rifle had "American Sniper" on one side and an American flag on the other. This rifle was able to shoot long distances. The fifth gun was a 308-pullback scope camouflaged with an estimated worth of ten thousand dollars. I think this was Chris's 308 sniper rifle or a replica of it.

All five guns were recovered at the crime scene. In a close-up picture, gun one had a magazine in it. None were loaded. "The media calls these weapons assault rifles. We call them sporting rifles," Ranger Adcock says.

The defense says to Ranger Adcock, "You don't know whether these guns are loaded or not loaded just by looking at them."

It's break time. Ranger Adcock is told to step down from the witness stand. The bailiff says, "All rise." The jury leaves, then the family, and finally us common folks and media leave.

The defense calls Jodi Routh, the defendant's mother, to testify. Again, I can't hear the questions the defense is asking because they are not using their mics, but Eddie's mother says, "I have lived in Lancaster, Texas, for twenty-five years at 220 West Sixth Street near Danes Avenue. I am married and have two children, Laura and Eddie. Eddie is twenty-seven and grew up in Lancaster before transferring to Midlothian, Texas."

Jodi Roth continues to tell the court about her son. "He made fair grades and played football. Eddie graduated in 2006 and came out of school as a private first class. He then went to Maryland and learned small arms weapons repair. Eddie hunted a lot and served in Iraq in 2007 and 2008."

She says, "Eddie went to Haiti on a humanitarian effort to clean debris for three months. He was stationed on the *USS Bataan* and spent seven months on the ship. He had no mental illness history. Eddie flew all over the United States to bases repairing guns."

Jodi matter-of-factly and seemingly without emotion tells the court, "Eddie was not his happy-go-lucky self he used to be. He spends time with his family, but has difficulties expressing his feelings. He watches what is going on but is very cautious. Eddie went to the Veterans Hospital in Dallas in 2011. He admitted himself because he thought he was suicidal. Eddie was on nine different medications and went to several group meetings. Every two weeks he went to see the doctor. In January 2013, he was admitted to Green Oaks Hospital and then transferred to a veteran's hospital. Eddie has one son and one daughter."

She tells the court, "On January 6, 2013, I asked Chris Kyle to work with Eddie. Chris came to talk to me, and I told Chris that Eddie was having trouble. Chris said that he would love to do anything he could for my son."

I notice while Eddie's mother is testifying that Eddie won't look at her. I find this very strange. After all, she is his mother. I feel her testimony is very cold and rehearsed.

Jodi Routh goes on to say, "I received a call at school, where I work, letting me know that the hospital was going to release Eddie. I objected and told the hospital that he was not ready. The hospital released Eddie, and he had Chris Kyle's phone number."

Jodi says that her husband had gone to live and work in Abilene, Texas. Her daughter lives in Cedar Hill, sixteen miles southwest of downtown Dallas. "I have Chris's phone number in my phone," she says. When asked about marijuana use, Jodi Routh answers, "Eddie and I have smoked marijuana together, and I do not think he abused it. It calmed him down."

At this point it has become known to the court that Eddie, his sister, and his mother all have smoked marijuana.

The district attorney stands to cross-examine. He asks Jodi, "What does Eddie hunt for?"

She replies, "Deer, rabbit, squirrels, and birds. He goes hunting with friends and family and took a gun safety course when he was twelve. He works on all guns up to a fifty caliber. He is a skilled shot. He was a prison guard in Iraq for seven months."

Jodi goes on to say, "Eddie spent seven months on a ship. He went to Haiti after the earthquake and tsunami and told me he cleaned up bodies off the beach."

The DA asks about the fish fry. She begins the story about the family fish fry. "My husband, Raymond, came home from Abilene, where he has a job with better opportunities. Eddie got into an argument with him. Eddie wanted his dad to sell some firearms so he could go to school. Raymond didn't want to sell them. Eddie ended being picked up by the police, but they took him to the hospital instead of jail. The police removed eight guns from the house where we were having the fish fry. Eddie had been drunk."

The DA asks Jodi what Eddie did, meaning his profession. She says, "He repaired guns on military bases for eight months. He has done lot of different jobs. Eddie was asked to work where they make cabinets. He lived with me and his dog, Girly."

The DA starts talking, saying, "The VA doctor wouldn't listen to Eddie. Eddie didn't like the hospital or the doctors. On January 26, he talked his mother into helping him get out of the hospital. Jodi met with Chris at school and asked him to help Eddie. She told Chris he had several hospital visits. Chris said he understood and knew what he was going through. Chris thought he could help Eddie. Within a week, Eddie had committed the two murders."

To me, it looks like Eddie's mother may have facilitated an early release for Eddie from the hospital. Jodi Routh seems cold and calculating. The DA made a point of saying that Eddie got a lump sum for back pay and medical expenses of $35,000. He also has a monthly income of $2,800 a month.

Day 6: Wednesday, February 18, 2015

Thinking back, the beginning of the trial was quite different as compared to now even though most of the law men and the crowd are mostly the same. There are some new lawyers and new lawmen who have come to observe, but as a whole, it is the same people. The trial has become relaxed a bit and not at all like the first three or four days, which were much more serious and intense. I mean, then, there was so much tension, you were afraid to pick your nose. All the officials were dead serious and expected everyone to sit perfectly still in their seat all day. If you were told to stop, you stopped. If you were told to move, you moved. If you left the courtroom, you could not come back in until the next break. It could just be me, but it seems more relaxed. Anyway, I feel a lot more comfortable being at the trial now.

Eddie is escorted in by three men. He is wearing a dark suit and blue shirt with a green and gray tie.

The defense calls Donna Taylor to the stand. She owns and operates the countertop and cabinet-making business where Eddie had been employed. She was born in Dallas but in 2006 moved to Waxahachie, Texas. She employs four full-time employees. She took Eddie home and picked him up for work.

She has been a lifelong friend of Jodi Routh, Eddie's mother. They had attended school together at Cedar Hill. Eddie went to school at Midlothian. "Eddie was bothered after he came back from Iraq," Donna states.

Donna has apparently done a lot for Eddie, and he never even looks up at her while she is testifying.

The district attorney now cross-examines Donna. She is not unattractive but rough looking, a tough-looking old gal who might whip your ass if crossed. The DA asks her if she smoked pot with Eddie and she answers, "On occasion. It helps me with my pain. I don't take prescription medication for pain."

The DA then mentions claims that they smoked marijuana at work. Donna says Eddie was around firearms all his life, and he qualified as a marksman in the marines. On February 1, the day before the murders, Donna dropped him off at his house after work. Eddie's mom and dad were out of town, and he had the house to himself. Donna says she is not aware he went out back and smoked pot at work. Eddie was frustrated at the VA hospital. Donna says, "Eddie threatened to kill his family and himself at the fish fry, so they took the guns out of the house. There were around six guns that belonged to Raymond, his father, who had inherited the antique guns. Eddie went to a mental hospital, and he had threatened his girlfriend with a knife."

The prosecution and defense attorneys don't use the microphones, so most of the time I can't hear their questions. The witnesses use them and their answers can be heard clearly. I know I sound like a broken record, but it is really aggravating.

The defense calls James Blevins to the stand. He is Laura Blevins's, Eddie's sister's, husband. They have three children—a six-year-old and a set of twins. James works for a fire protection company. He knew Eddie while he was in the military. On February 2, 2013, between 5:00 and 6:00 pm, James was at his house. A little after 5:00, Eddie called to say he was coming over. James said it was between 5:30 and 5:45 when Eddie arrived. James was on the couch, and it was a nice day. The door was open, and Eddie walked in. James says *Eddie* seemed not to be there. Eddie said, "Is it just me, or is the world freezing over?" James says that the hair on the back of his neck stood up. Eddie then said he had taken two souls, and James had a sick feeling. Laura asked what he meant, and Eddie said he shot two people. James said, "Get help, call the police." Eddie offered to show them the guns in the truck. James said, "You need to go." He asked Eddie if he traded his VW for the pickup. Eddie said he traded his soul for the pickup. Laura called the police.

The DA stands to cross-examine James and asks, "What did you do, James?"

James replies, "We went to the police station to file a report about the conversation."

Eddie mentioned to James and Laura that he had killed two people and was going to run to Oklahoma. James wanted Eddie to leave. He said, "Just get in the truck and leave." James says then they went to the police station to make a report. The defense asks James if he smelled marijuana smoke or if Eddie was drunk. James had not noticed either. James is excused from the stand and steps down.

The defense calls Laura Blevins to the stand. Laura says Eddie is her little brother and there is a three-year difference in their ages. She says Eddie was an average student and they have had regular conversations since he got out of the marines. They still see each other fairly regularly. On February 2, 2013, Eddie called Laura, and she didn't want to answer the phone because of Jen Weed and how Eddie had gotten himself put back in the Green Oak Hospital for pulling a knife on her. Eddie walked into their house saying *pigs were sucking on his soul*. Eddie sat at her table and said he killed two guys at the gun range and he had taken their souls before they took his. Laura says she told him, "You can't just kill someone. You have to turn yourself in." When Laura saw what Eddie was driving, she knew that he couldn't afford that truck. She told Eddie, "I hate your demons."

At 10:00 there is a break. Everyone rises, and then the jury, the family, and the rest of us leave in that order.

It sure feels good not to be sitting right now. It hurts me to sit for long periods of time. My butt and back bother me a lot, being four-year survivor of colon cancer. Sometimes I am in a lot of pain.

I am milling around outside the courtroom, and I see two new Texas Rangers. Both are tall, nice-looking black men. They are slim and trim and ready to go. All the rangers I see are the real deal and full of pride. This elite group of men, along with the Texas Highway Patrol, are the force that keeps this trial free of disruption. If chaos were to break out, the rangers are best qualified to take control of a situation before it gets out of hand.

I ask one of the rangers who was about six foot five and shorter than the others, "How tall is that ranger over there?"

He tells me, "He is only five foot nine. The hat just makes him look tall." That was pretty funny. He then says, "He is really six foot seven. There are no restrictions on height in the Texas Rangers organization."

All the rangers I see here have better-than-average looks and muscular builds. I ask him if it is an advantage being tall and if it helps them when shooting by being able to see over most obstacles. He says it can work both ways and that an advantage can also be a disadvantage. Speaking to the ranger is a welcome break from the trial.

Court takes up session, and Laura Blevins is still on the stand being questioned by the DA about issues prior to February 2, 2013. On September 12 Eddie and his dad had gotten into an argument about the guns in the house. Eddie didn't go to jail; he went to the hospital. In January 2013, Jen Weed and Eddie got in an argument. Eddie again went to the hospital instead of jail. Laura knew he could not afford that pickup truck. She told authorities that Eddie killed two people. She called 911 and later wrote out a statement. Eddie was making statements that *pigs were in his soul and coming out of him*. He was going to Oklahoma to get out of this mess. The whole family had smoked pot or did smoke pot according to what Laura said.

The defense cross-examines her and wants to know the total time Eddie was at Laura's house. She replies about fifteen minutes. During her 911 call to the police, she said that Eddie was "fucking psycho." Laura says there are two Eddies—the nice one she grew up with and the psycho. She said on the 911 call he was psycho.

The defense calls Jennifer Weed to the stand. She is twenty-six years old and has two younger brothers. She has a degree in psychology. Jen and Eddie met on a dating website in April or May. Jen says that they spent a lot of time outdoors. They went hunting together. In May of 2011 they decided that they would date each other exclusively. Jen never saw Eddie take his medication but knew he was prescribed medicine. In her opinion "he smoked a lot of pot." Jen says in September 2012 everyone was drinking at the fish fry, and Eddie ended up in the psychological part of the hospital.

Jennifer Weed and Eddie Routh were beginning to get on each other's nerves. Eddie moved back home with his mother. On January 19, Jen got a call that Eddie was upset. She went to pick him up from his mother's house, and then they got into an argument with each other. Eddie was calling Jennifer names and wanted to go back home. She talked him into spending the night at her place.

The next morning Eddie broke out in a sweat that soaked his shirt. He then began to have another spell and ended up pulling a knife on her. The police were called, and he went to the hospital instead of jail.

On January 27, 2013, Eddie was released and went back to his mother's house.

On February 1, 2013, Jen went to see Eddie. She found him sitting out back next door with Greg, the neighbor, smoking pot. Jen started playing with Girly, Eddie's dog. She hated it when he smoked. Eddie had promised that he would stop smoking and drinking. Later, after they were back inside, Eddie started hallucinating and thought the government was listening to their conversation. Jennifer explained on the stand that Eddie would go weeks without showering. Jen was helping him fill out paperwork for a Waco hospital, and she and Eddie started fighting. Jen called Uncle James to come over. After Uncle James arrived, she left to have lunch with her mom. James later sent Jen a text telling her Eddie just left with Chris Kyle. The defense asks if she knew that Chris was coming over to pick up Eddie on February 2, 2013. She says she didn't know about that.

Mrs. Starnes with the prosecution stands and begins cross-examination by asking Jen Weed about her time working in the DA's office in Dallas on long-term disability claims and about Eddie and her meeting on a dating website called Plenty of Fish. There was a standing joke that I didn't get or didn't hear right. "Jen Weed got (or caught) some last night." This statement was brought up and there were some snickers in the courtroom, but I'm still not sure I get it.

Jen went on to say that Eddie drove a VW Bug called Lady Bug. Eddie thought he would have a rabbit and goat farm, but at that time he was mowing lawns for a realtor. She went on to say he wasn't a stylish guy and they hunted and fished together. He was a good shot. They didn't go out much. Eddie had been a prison guard and had a quick temper over little things. Early on the day of the fish fry they had gone fishing. While at the fish fry, he threatened to kill his family and himself and was sent to Green Oaks Hospital instead of going to jail. Jen says she is against marijuana and has had family members impacted by the effects of marijuana.

Jen states that on January 19, 2013, Eddie was worried about losing his soul. He needed to quit smoking and drinking and had started to slow down. Eddie thought he was going to die that night. The next morning, he wanted to go see his attorney. He was supposed to look up the address of the attorney and go to see him, but he was afraid to leave the house. Eddie went to the kitchen and got a knife out of the butcher block. He was waving it around. Jen's roommate, Gabby, was getting ready to go to work. Gabby and Jen tried to calm Eddie down. Gabby had a policeman friend who she worked with, so she called him. The policeman showed up, and Gabby escaped. The policeman took him to the hospital. Jen Weed says that Eddie told the doctor that he could make more money in construction than the doctor could in a day's work. She continues by saying that the day Eddie got out of the VA hospital, she found him smoking pot with Greg the neighbor.

On February 1, 2013, Jen Weed got off work and found Eddie

in the backyard at Greg's house smoking pot. She told them if they offered the glass pipe to her, she would break it.

Greg said, "If you break it you owe me eighty dollars."

She told him, "Ok, but if you give it to me I'll break it."

Jen was carrying Eddie's medication with her and trying to make sure he took it on time. Eddie thought they ought to start making pot cupcakes. Jen then shares that she and Eddie went to bed together and had sex. They got up in the morning and started fighting over a can of snuff. Jen didn't like tobacco either. She sent a text to James saying, "If you don't get over here, I am going to kill your nephew." She left the house when Uncle James Watson showed up.

Jen says, "I put myself in harm's way to take care of Eddie."

That is the end of Jen Weed's testimony, and the sixth day of the trial is over. It is time for me to get something to eat and go to bed. Four o'clock a.m. comes early, and my ass is killing me from sitting. I might go to Jake and Dorothy's Café, where they have dollar hamburgers, thirty-five types of pies, and twenty-six different kinds of cakes, all made from scratch. Then it's back to the Motel 6—you know, where they leave the light on for you.

Day 7: Thursday, February 19, 2015

Today is the seventh day of the trial, Thursday, February 19, 2015. I notice Mr. Kyle, Chris's father, has the little finger on his left hand missing at the joint. He is an average-looking red-blooded American who has had his heart torn out by Eddie Routh and this trial.

Eddie is wearing a dark suit, blue shirt, and red tie. I don't know who it is, but there is definitely someone dressing Eddie each day of this trial. The look is very pretentious considering what we have learned of his character so far. The jury is not yet present. The defense and the prosecution are arguing before the judge about the word *wrong*. The jury is not yet in the courtroom.

The defense calls their witness, Dr. Major Charles Overstreet, to the stand. He states that he teaches social courses. He was in the army for twelve years with Operation Freedom stationed in Iraq and is a major mental health provider. On March 14, 2014, he was asked to go to the jail to see a veteran who was accused of murder—Eddie Routh. The interview lasted three and a half hours during separate sessions. Dr. Overstreet reviewed Eddie's medical records and medications. Dr. Overstreet testifies that Eddie was suffering from a mental disorder and didn't know at the time of the murders what he was doing was wrong.

The DA stands and states, "Dr. Overstreet has no license, suffers from a mental disease, and is not familiar with Texas laws. Dr. Overstreet uses the word *wrong* and states 'did not know his actions were wrong.' The word *wrong* is not described in the Texas penal code." The DA says, "Did Eddie describe if Chad had a weapon in his hand? Eddie misinterpreted why Chad and Chris were there. Eddie fired on Chad, then turned and shot Chris several times. Eddie planned to kill both of them while riding in the truck on the way to the shooting range." The DA proclaims, "There was no range master, and no one else was at the range. Dr. Overstreet's job is to access the situation and prescribe the help the patient needs."

Dr. Major Overstreet is disqualified and will not be testifying.

The DA calls Dr. Mitchell H. Dunn, introduces him, and takes his statement that he had seen Eddie professionally between March 6 and November 12, 2013. Dr. Dunn is then asked to be seated.

The jury is brought in, and I look over at Taya. Today she is wearing black pants and a brown tweed jacket.

The defense calls Jodi Routh to the stand. Jodi, Eddie's mother, says she had talked to Chris before Eddie got out of the hospital. Jodi Routh worked as an assistant in the school that Chris and Taya's children attend. They show pictures taken the day her daughter, Laura, was married and pictures of Eddie in his uniform with his mother. Eddie was twenty years old in the picture. He was eighteen when he joined the marines and left for boot camp.

The DA approaches to cross-examine. When asked, Jodi says she "never advised Chris that Eddie went back to the hospital"!

"Chris Kyle didn't know all that had gone down before he picked Eddie up the morning of February 2, 2013! It had not occurred to Jodi Routh that all that information could have saved Chris Kyle's life. It never occurred to her!" the district attorney says and then sits down.

The defense stands and shows a picture of Eddie and Jen Weed to compare the physical appearance of Eddie when he was in the marines to later with Jennifer Weed.

The defense calls Dr. Mitchell Dunn to the stand. He relates that he did his internship in psychology, was board certified in psychiatry, and worked at the state mental hospital in Terrell, Texas. The jury is told that Dr. Dunn has been called to evaluate whether Eddie is competent to stand trial and if he does or does not understand what is going on. Dr. Dunn starts talking, and it goes something like this. There are ninety-six legal systems that require someone to be sane or insane. He has been evaluating people who commit crimes for twenty years. He has been around people who commit crimes for twenty years and has found them to be sane at the time of the charge. He starts talking about mental illness and elements of psychosis, a break in reality, also known as psychotic disorder. According to the Mayo Clinic, a disconnection from reality hallucination or phantosmia makes you detect smells. In March of 2013, the five senses of delusion—vision, hearing, smell, taste, and touch—and common positive symptoms of psychosis were invalid with Eddie. Dr. Dunn says you try to go in as objective as possible when interviewing a person. Green Oaks Psychiatric Hospital, operating for twenty-five years as an inpatient and outpatient chemical dependency hospital, reviewed their report and crime scene photos on April 15, 2014. Dr. Dunn says he had six hours and fifteen minutes of nontypical questions about information he had reviewed today of the offense records. In 2011 at the beginning of Eddie Routh's records from the VA Hospital, it was determined that psychotic disorder, bipolar, and PTSD needed further study. Eddie was diagnosed as a psychotic in 2011. He admitted himself for a tape worm that he thought he had. He was diagnosed with a psychosis or psychotic disorder because it was a false belief. He was prescribed an antidepressant stabilizer, antipsychotics, and sleep medication. Another visit to the hospital was brought on because of the fish fry incident when Eddie threatened to kill his family and himself. Instead of going to jail, he was repeatedly sent to the hospital. He had a dependency on alcohol and marijuana. In 2013 he was hospitalized again when he held Jennifer Weed and her friend at knifepoint. He was again diagnosed as having a psychotic disorder. Eddie was released from the hospital on January 25.

The defense is trying really hard to prove Eddie has a history of some real mental problems. After all, this is their only defense for committing the murders.

Dr. Dunn goes on to speak about a marijuana high. He says a normal high on marijuana will last two to three hours, but according to Dr. Dunn, a user will test positive for a week to a month depending on how often it is smoked.

Eddie raises his head up from the table where he has been doodling. This is what he has done during the entire trial—doodling while everyone else is carrying on with the trial. I would like to look at his doodles.

Eddie's mental status, emotional state, MoCA test, cognitive test, and McLean Test were studied to determine if he was faking disorders. Dr. Dunn sees some effect of psychosis, delusional thinking, and paranoia. For example, he thought that his neighbor was a member of the Mexican Mafia. Dr. Dunn thinks this is why he drew a knife and a neighbor's sword on his girlfriend and her friend. At work, he thought the food the employees ate at the cabinet shop didn't look right. He thought they were cannibals and were eating human flesh. He thought the heaters in the cabinet shop were there to cook and eat him. Eddie's head is still up, paying close attention to what is being said.

Dr. Dunn states, "A lot of people who have this disease are pretty much normal if they take their medication regularly."

Psychiatry is the study and treatment of mental illness, emotional disturbance, and abnormal behavior according to Oxford Dictionaries.[2] Wikipedia defines it as the medical specialty devoted to the study, diagnosis, treatment, and prevention of mental disorders. These include various affective behavioral actions and cognitive and perceptual abnormalities. [3]

According to Wikipedia, which agrees and is in line with Webster, psychology is the study of the mind and behavior. It is an academic discipline in an applied science that seeks to understand individuals and groups by establishing general principles and researching specific

---
[2] https://en.oxforddictionaries.com/definition/psychiatry
[3] https://en.wikipedia.org/wiki/Psych

cases. Psychologists evaluate and study of behavior and mental processes.

Every morning the Kyle family is police escorted in a motor procession to the south parking lot of the Donald R. Jones Justice Center in Stephenville. Every evening after court adjourns the police escort the family from the door of the justice center to their vehicles, and the motor procession leaves in the direction it came from with lights flashing.

Many of the lawmen and bailiff look like ex-boxers. The lawmen are in the front, back, middle, and both sides of the judge in the courtroom.

Jim Walton, a Vietnam veteran who I became friends with during my stay in Stephenville, told me this about life during service and life after serving in the military. Jim said, "In the army or any other military branch, every day is a big deal. It is life or death, but when you come back to the States, nothing is as crucial as war and life's perspectives change. It can be a letdown when things are not as important and intense all of a sudden. An adjustment to everyday life is required."

The defense is still interrogating Dr. Dunn about things that Eddie has said, like, "Jennifer Weed's ears weren't the same. They can live a somewhat normal life, half man, half kids, half pigs. Pigs are taking over the earth." He talked about the color of his snot. Eddie had told Dr. Dunn he was eating his own excrement. Dr. Dunn said that Eddie would go many days without bathing. Eddie had drunk whiskey and smoked weed before Chris Kyle picked him up. Eddie was tired of everyone's shit. He did not like the odor of Chris's truck. He thought the ride with Chris and Chad was a one-way trip and two white cars were following them. Chris and Eddie were shooting, but Chad wasn't. Eddie told Dr. Dunn he thought that was weird. He shot Chad as Chris was turning, and then he shot Chris. Dr. Dunn asked Eddie if he thought they were going to kill him, why they'd given him a gun. Dr. Dunn got no answer to this question from Eddie.

Dr. Dunn is going over what Eddie had told him about what had happened to him that day. Eddie thought he was acting in self-defense. Seems like he made a mistake. Eddie was thinking this was not going to look good and that if he was going to be arrested, he had better get something to eat. That was why he stopped at the Taco Bell. He should have called the police at the gun range, but he made it to I-35 northbound and got T-boned.

Dr. Dunn's opinion is that Eddie was going through a severe case of schizophrenia or disorganized thinking. Eddie was saying things that were disconnected. Dr. Dunn feels like the schizophrenia started in July of 2011. Dr. Dunn points out that Chris and Chad realized there was something else wrong with Eddie other than PTSD when they texted each other in the truck, "This guy is straight up nuts. Watch my six."

Dr. Dunn said that there are approximately twenty million people in the United States who smoke pot, and they generally do not experience this type of behavior. A drug psychosis happens while you are intoxicated. Eddie was still thinking this way in April.

The district attorney gets up and starts talking to Dr. Dunn and says at the time the defendant was charged, his conduct was a result of severe mental disease or the defendant did not know that his conduct was wrong. Insanity in the Texas Penal Code Section 8.01 Texas Law (a) says, "It is an affirmative defense to prosecution that, at the time of the conduct charged, the actor, as a result of severe mental disease or defect, did not know that his conduct was wrong. (b) The term 'mental disease or defect' does not include an abnormality manifested only by repeated criminal or otherwise antisocial conduct."

The district attorney continues to cross-examine the defense's witness, Dr. Dunn. The DA says Dr. Dunn received almost all of Eddie's medical reports but he didn't review all the mail coming to and from jail and never saw school records or the DUI report from 2012. He also never talked to doctors at the VA Hospital. He charges $400 an hour plus travel expenses to testify as an expert witness. Dr. Dunn wasn't present at the auditory evaluation, the most common type of psychosis. The DA adds, "I have in my notes that in 2011 during Eddie's first hospital visit he tested positive for pot and formaldehyde. Eddie's second visit to the hospital, he had delusions of a tapeworm. He was dehydrated, which was probably the cause for the visit. In 2012 during the fish fry incident, he was drunk and threatened everyone's life. Every time he went to the hospital, he tested positive for marijuana. On January 19, the Waco, Texas, program that Eddie was trying to get admitted to would not accept him without being sober. This was the program that Jen Weed was working on the day of the murders. Dr. Dunn said that it is hard to make a diagnosis of a patient without the subject being sober. Dr. Dunn stated, 'People lie to doctors.' On February 2013 Eddie lied to Dr. Dunn about using marijuana, thinking it would affect the data a doctor records for a mental analysis."

In order to get disability, Eddie listed every body part he had as having something wrong with it. Four days before he saw Dr. Dunn, Eddie had watched the show *Boss Hog*. Dr. Dunn called it hogology. Eddie had a policeman for a neighbor. According to Dr. Dunn, Eddie told him his whole family would go outside on the back porch and smoke. Eddie made a disparaging comment about people who were not white. During all this he worked at the cabinet shop.

Dr. Dunn says it is rare that people have weird smells with schizophrenia. We don't know what Chris Kyle meant by the word *nuts*. Chris and Chad didn't talk much to Eddie on the way to the lodge. Eddie was pretty sure Chad had a gun and said he shot Chad again because he was moving around. A reasonable defense is a cause for self-protection—a right to defend things. Eddie said, "I had to shoot two guys." He told Dr. Dunn, "In the Bible it says not to kill. Pretty shitty thing to do, to kill someone." He figured he would be arrested, so Eddie bought the burritos because he knew he was going to jail. "This is not going to look good," Eddie said. He knew it was bad.

Eddie fled the scene. It was 105 miles from the lodge to Lancaster. He loaded the 9 mm and armed himself before he left the lodge. He left his sister's house when she told him she called the police. He said, "I am going to Oklahoma to get out of this mess." He knew he was in a mess. Some people believe it is right to cut heads off, and some believe it is right to put a bomb in your underwear. To shoot someone seven times, you want that person dead. That doesn't make it right. We don't make our own laws.

Besides what is listed, here are the things he did or did not do. He didn't call the police, he went to the Dollar Store to buy a Dr. Pepper, and he went to his sister's house. He knew he was in trouble when he was at his house surrounded by police being begged by the officer who he knew to turn over Chris's truck and get out. The truck finally quit running on I-35 headed to Oklahoma, and Eddie knew when it stopped to get out with his hands up and lie on the ground.

The DA, still reviewing statements from the trial so far, says that Eddie smoked marijuana before and after dinner every day after he got out of the marines. Eddie was the only one thinking he was threatened at the lodge with Chris and Chad. Eddie thought his training was better than Chris's training. Eddie had some narcissism in him. He shot Chad first but didn't tell the doctor he shot him in the back.

Eddie's military records had not one stress-related symptom mentioned in them. Eddie felt anger, envy, and jealousy. Eddie was perplexed that Chris didn't shake his hand. He told officers he killed them because they didn't talk to him on the way to the shooting range. He felt he wasn't treated as special as he thought he should have been.

He drove a VW Beatle that was painted to look like a ladybug. Dr. Dunn considered this an example of low self-esteem. He could feel good about himself by killing the American Sniper.

The DA says, "The law in Texas says nothing about temporary insanity."

The defense rises and has some questions or statements at this time. Believing your life is in harm's way is self-defense. Eddie felt he had been in danger all day. When he got locked up, Eddie felt safe. Dr. Dunn thinks that the statement "everybody is eating on my soul" is very telling. Dr. Dunn says these statements are signs of mental illness. "I have been having panic attacks all day," the defense says, quoting Eddie.

In my opinion, I think that if I had viciously attacked two people and shot them up the way Eddie did for no reason I would be having panic attacks all day too.

The test for marijuana that came out of Eddie's house proved to be straight marijuana. "Some of the doctors said he had PTSD," the defense remarks. "Dr. Dunn does not believe this."

The district attorney says that senseless crimes happen every day, and some are justified. It is hard to live with yourself knowing you are a cold-blooded killer.

The defense speaks up and says that Dr. Davis thinks Eddie did these things because he is insane.

The jury is excused, and the defense tells Eddie he has the right to testify. Eddie does not want to testify.

The defense calls Dr. Davis to the stand and asks, "According to the Texas Penal Code 801, Dr. Davis, do you think Eddie Routh was insane when he committed these crimes?"

Dr. Davis replies, "Yes." Dr. Davis is excused, and the defense introduces their next witness, Dr. Randall Price.

It is obvious now that the jury has been let go for the rest of the evening. I suppose that is best due to the weather conditions since it has been slightly warmer today and when nightfall comes the roads will likely freeze over again.

Dr. Randall Price takes the stand and states that he got his forensic psychology degree at North Texas University and his doctorate at

Baylor. Dr. Price viewed the jail files, transcripts, video tape, autopsy reports, and state of the witness investigation report and the ranger crime scene file from Lancaster, Texas. Dr. Price did six hours of tests and interviews on January 24. He analyzed the records and information, and his diagnostic opinion at the time was a cannabis-induced psychosis.

The defense next introduces Michael Alegria, doctor of pharmacy. Dr. Alegria was in private practice in Chicago for one year and was a consultant in civil cases. He looked at Eddie Routh's records on January 30, 2015. The DA asks Dr. Alegria how long he has been a pharmacist. He says, "Eight years, and I am board certified in psychology."

The trial ends for the day.

Day 8: February 20, 2015

This is Friday, the eighth day of the trial, February 20, 2015. The weather is warming up today, but Tuesday, Wednesday, and Thursday were extremely cold. Waiting in line to enter the courtroom has been brutal because there is nothing but a barbed wire fence stopping the north wind, which has been blowing about thirty miles per hour. The chill factor has been severe. I have been wearing gloves, thermals under my suit, and a heavy coat and have still been freezing.

The Donald R. Jones Justice Center on that freezing February day.

There are several remote news trucks still here and as usual a line of people trying to get into the courtroom. The parking lot across from the justice center is filled with media trucks. I see NBC, CBS, ABC, FOX, and CNN, and there are probably more here covering this trial. Stephenville has made the big-time with this trial being publicized on national news. There is one guy who has been filming the trial from outside the courtroom through the glass on the door. He has no sound that I know of unless there is a mic that I cannot see. It is a sad trial for such a true hero and family man to be gunned down that way. You can hear laughter and cackling sounds coming from the people in line, but to me it is too sad to be joyful about anything. They let the family in first, then the news people, then people like me.

Media trucks set up near the justice center.

Taya Kyle is wearing dark blue jeans with a diamond-patterned black nylon jacket and a royal blue blouse, knee-high boots, and black-rimmed glasses. She is composed as always and nods and smiles a little at friends and family as she makes her way to her seat.

Eddie has on a dark suit and blue shirt with a gray-green brown striped tie. He struts and sways into the room as usual, seeming to avoid all eye contact.

The DA calls Officer Stewart to the stand. They play a recorded phone call between Eddie and Nicholas Schmidle, author of the article "In the Crosshairs." Eddie says in an excited tone that he is "doing excellent and trying to do ten years of writing." Eddie says, "The food is good, and I need to be talking to you. I need to get out. I was in Baghdad in 2007 and 2008 from September to March. I did a year in the Mediterranean. I need to talk to a writer." This was on a Monday at 3:00 on April 24. Eddie said he had cable TV and his bond was three million dollars. Sergeant Stewart steps down, and the next witness was called.

Listening to that recording makes me think that Eddie is dreaming of fame.

The DA calls Dr. Randel Price, who has been a chemical psychologist for thirty years. He explains he has a doctorate of psychology and taught for forty-three years as a college professor and is a board-certified forensic psychologist. He comes to court to testify on civil and criminal cases. He is familiar with the term *insanity* and states that he looks at the big picture—the before, during, and after. In March 2013, he became acquainted with Eddie Routh's case. He had looked pretty much at all of the files on Eddie to the present. He went with the DA to talk to other doctors who had seen Eddie and received a court order on October 2014 to talk to Eddie. On December 5, 2014, he went to the jail to meet with Eddie in a multipurpose room with one-way mirrors, which are called panels. He conducted a four and one-half hour interview with Eddie, and with his consent, he also did some testing. Dr. Price says Mr. Routh has somewhat of an attention problem. He returned on January 16, 2015, for a five- to six-hour interview.

Dr. Price said during general conversation, Eddie showed obsessive behavior mental status. Typically, during a clinical interview, the prospective expectation of events leading up to the offense is bent toward the accused's version of what happened before, during, and after, comparing results to other people's accounts. Defendants have a tendency to guide the information given on their own behalf.

The question is "Was the defendant insane at the time of the assault?"

Dr. Price says, "He does not meet the state of insanity or voluntary intoxication altered mental state. He did know what he was doing was wrong, and he did it anyway." Dr. Price disagrees with Dr. Dunn. "Eddie was not experiencing schizophrenia. It was malingering information. Eddie was big fan of *Seinfeld* and there is a scene where Cramer believed he saw a one-half man and one-half pig or a pig man—a boss hog hybrid of men and pigs. When Eddie talked, he did a lot of comparing pigs to people. His diagnosis at the time of the murder would be different now since he has been in jail in a completely different environment with no access to pot and alcohol. Also, since for two years he has been taking his medicine regularly, he would not be in the same state of mind that he was on February 2, 2013. During the offense, his condition was different, and he had personality disorders, adjustment disorders, substance-induced psychotic disorder, cannabis disorder, and alcohol use disorder" (new term for drunk).

"Personality disorder is a pattern in people's lives. They handle things all dependent. They have problems in making decisions. Paranoid personality disorder is always thinking one is being taken advantage of," explains Dr. Price. "You can't trust other people and hold grudges. Often a person will think a spouse is cheating on him or her and become angry at other people easily. A personality disorder is not the same as a mental disorder. Paranoid personality disorder heightens the paranoia and suspicion of others and causes anger easily. The most trouble seen adjusting and acting out happens when your job is not satisfying.

"Eddie's adjustment disorder is evident because Eddie was not getting to do what he wanted to do in the marines. When he got out of the marines, he was not satisfied with what he was doing, and it troubled him from then until now."

Dr. Price states, "Pot is a totally harmless problem, as is alcohol. It is a safe substance when used in moderation. Small percentages of people become dependent on pot, which then becomes a problem. Occasional marijuana use is maybe once on a weekend, and heavy is getting up every morning and smoking a joint. This starts causing a problem in your life because you do not want to do anything, so the users isolate themselves."

As we used to say in college, you just want to sit in a corner and grow your hair long. I grew up in the '60s, graduating high school in 1968. I now realize that the pot today is way different than what we smoked back then, so I guess I agree with the doctor. As strong as the pot is today, I don't think I would be having a good time with it.

The doctor continued. "THC is the most common drug of cannabis. The potency of marijuana in 1980 was 4 percent THC and in 2012 it was 15 percent. Cannabis psychosis is rarely induced by marijuana. Heightened senses, increased appetite, and paranoia are effects of marijuana use, along with panic attack, fear of dying, distortion of time, and visual distortion. Drugs on the street don't have labels. Pleasant and unpleasant effects disturb thought processes. The effects last longer than intoxication. It is like starting a fire in your BBQ pit. The high is the charcoal lighter fuel. Once it burns out, the coals keep going. People can act normal and be intoxicated." Dr. Price does not think Eddie is psychotic. Combining alcohol and pot intensifies the intoxication effect. His alcohol abuse disorder progressed in the marines and probably started in high school. "Cannabis abuse makes one irritable and depressed. It also causes a heightened sense of light that seems brighter and sounds that are louder."

Dr. Price continues, "Eddie used the word *soul* a lot. *Taking souls* and *suck souls* is a pattern of speech, as is smoking in the mirror or smoking mirrors as a metaphor. Eddie saw a lot of non-American doctors that he didn't like. Eddie said he didn't like a railroad coming through the hospital, meaning you are railroading me. During the phone call he received in jail thirteen days after his arrest, his speech was responsive, not disjointed, and his thinking was clear. The big difference was his conversation was much clearer since he had been sober for thirteen days. It was a vast improvement."

On December 15 and January 16, the Montreal Cognitive Assessment tests found Eddie to have average intelligence except his attention level scored lower. Dr. Price said that Eddie tried to fake conditions on the SIMS Test. No pigs came up during that examination. He lied to receive disability. When asked to check below if you have a problem, he checked every body part on the bone diagram page. On the personality disorder results, he showed paranoid and narcissistic traits and believed he should be treated better. Eddie believed several people were jealous of him because he was tall, handsome, and a marine. Eddie had problems with anxiety, drugs, and alcohol.

In answers to questions prior to 2013, Eddie denied having a drug problem, and six months before, in his opinion, he did not have PTSD.

The next part of the testing showed Eddie talking a lot about his life history. His alcohol and marijuana use started in his adolescence. He drank a lot in the marines but didn't smoke marijuana because they drug tested, and if you tested positive, you were kicked out. He said he smoked pot the night before the murders but didn't use the day of, which was not true according to his uncle's testimony, which stated that they had smoked two bowls and drank whiskey thirty minutes before Chris picked him up on the morning of February 2, 2013.

Dr. Price continues, saying Eddie's military service work ranged from being a prison guard in Iraq to being on a ship in the Mediterranean sent to Haiti for disaster relief, to fixing guns and keeping inventory of small arms. He had no combat experience and didn't like his prison guard job. Eddie wanted to go into combat, and it made him mad that he did not get to. During the trip to Haiti, he experienced an earthquake that rolled the ship pretty good. He stayed on the ship monitoring equipment coming and going. Eddie only left the ship to get his paycheck because you got more money offshore.

One time Eddie and another guy thought they saw a dead body. He embellished by telling gruesome stories that he had piled up bodies of men and babies in Haiti.

On January 30, 2013, Eddie remained angry. The VA was not helping him collect education benefits. A home loan would pay for the trade school he wanted to go to, and the VA wouldn't give him a home loan.

On February 1, 2013, Eddie went to work, came home, and had drinks and marijuana then got up easily around 4:30 a.m. on February 2 and ate breakfast. He couldn't sleep. He tried to fill out paperwork for the rehab hospital but had to be sober before they would admit him. Eddie didn't want to get sober. Jen Weed bitched at him for dipping Copenhagen snuff, drinking, and smoking pot. His uncle, James Watson, came over, and they drank whiskey and coffee. Eddie was aggravated about the VA and his girlfriend.

Honoring his promise to Jodi Routh to meet with her son Eddie, around 1:00 p.m. on February 2, 2013, Chris Kyle picked Eddie Routh up from his house. He was surprised to see Chad Littlefield was with Chris. Both men told Eddie to get in, and he did. Eddie was surprised when he found out they were going to a shooting range. There were a lot of guns and ammunition in the truck, and this bothered him. They stopped at a Whataburger to get something to eat. Eddie was given a hamburger, but he wasn't hungry. Eddie got mad when neither Chris nor Chad shook his hand. Eddie said he tried to talk to them, but neither one would talk to him. This made him mad. Eddie was thinking, *I got to do something. I got to get out of this.* When they were at the range and Chad was not shooting, this made Eddie mad also.

He said, "So I shot Chad first. When I shot them, I thought, *Jesus Christ, what have I done.* Chad was quivering, so I walked over and shot him again. I didn't plan it. I shot the target facing me first. I shot targets facing me first and shot the targets facing away second." Eddie said that he only used a 9 mm to shoot both. Eddie said the attorney was wrong. He said the coroner did a fucked-up job. Eddie didn't admit he shot Chad seven times. Eddie left out a lot of information in order to tell his side of the story. In Dr. Price's opinion, these actions did not lead to a level of insanity.

Eddie considered shooting Chad and Chris on the way to the shooting range but was afraid they would have a wreck and he might get hurt. He shot Chad in the head so he couldn't get up.

Eddie told his sister and his brother-in-law that he "traded his soul for his new truck."

"That is a chronic mistrust of people," remarks Dr. Price. "He fled Rough Creek Lodge to Lancaster, Texas. He then got burritos because he was going to be arrested soon."

During Ranger Briley's interrogation, Eddie said, "It was a pretty shitty thing to do, killing someone. It tells you in the Bible not to kill." The speech of Eddie at the time of the arrest was schizophrenic. "I don't have much insight of prior arrest," Eddie said as he got out of the truck. He told police without being asked, "I am a marine and have PTSD."

The defense makes a point at this time to remind the jury that Dr. Price is getting paid $250 an hour and there is a mountain of evidence about Eddie in this case. The defense wants the jury to know that on March 13, 2013, Mr. Nash, the DA, had a meeting with eight to ten rangers who had handled some part of the evidence against Eddie Routh. The DA was really involved in this case and produced a report that was incomplete. The DA was thinking there might be new information that could come forth as it is a difficult case to diagnose. Psychiatrists may have different opinions when making a diagnosis. When making a diagnosis, you need as much information as you can get.

The defense continues. During Eddie's teen years, there were no psychosis symptoms found. In July of 2011 the first sign of psychosis appeared because of cannabis abuse. Five days later he was diagnosed again with psychosis. In September 2012, he was prescribed major antipsychotic medication. The doctor ruled out bipolar disorder. Eddie couldn't stay sober long enough to make a proper diagnosis of cannabis-induced psychosis. On February 2, 2013, Eddie had an episode under the influence of marijuana. The defense states, "There is not a test to prove you are under the influence of marijuana." The doctors say there are different mental and personality disorders that remain for a long time. Eddie talked in metaphors, using the word *soul*. He went to his uncle's and sister's houses around 3:30 to 4:30 after the killing occurred. The doctor states Eddie was under the influence when Ranger Briley interrogated him.

The defense points out that Eddie seemed relaxed and not paranoid or psychotic and asks, "Was he still on a cannabis-induced psychotic episode?" The defense, looking right at the jury about three feet in front of them, say, "No, didn't seem to be" in a loud voice.

The doctor says, "Eddie always maintained he shot both men with a 9-mm handgun."

The DA stands up with fire in his eyes. "The only reason Eddie keeps saying one gun killed both of them is because it looks better than using two guns. Acute and chronic cognitive thinking is still affected after a cannabis high has gone away. Eddie was very familiar with firearms. Eddie's personality disorder goes back to when he was in school and easily angered."

The defense says that for possession of marijuana thirty years ago you could go to prison for any amount of the substance. Now some states have legalized marijuana. Psychotic episodes due to cannabis are rare, and they are more common with the use of hard drugs. The defense continues saying that any quantity of hard drugs is a felony. Marijuana calmed Eddie down.

The DA remarks that the combination of marijuana and alcohol make some users get angry.

The DA calls Dr. Michael Arambula, MD. He has two degrees, a BS and doctorate of pharmacy and a doctorate of medicine from Santa Monica. He works as a pharmacist and is board certified in psychiatry and forensic psychology. He was a MD in Pasadena, Texas, for twenty years on the forensic medical board, appointed by Governor Perry. The DA asks the doctor what that paid. The doctor replies that it is $3,000 a day; his normal rate is $300 per hour plus travel expenses up to $200. One of his jobs is applying medical principles to legal cases by rehabilitating inmates back into society. Dr. Michael Arambula was familiar with this case and the records of Eddie Routh. It was his opinion that Eddie was not insane because he was intoxicated when the murders happened. Dr. Arambula says Eddie knew it was wrong. He also does not believe he has psychotic symptoms. He thinks Eddie's symptoms were drug induced because all drug tests performed on Eddie were positive except one. Eddie refused a urine analysis. Dr. Arambula explains that wet marijuana—which is marijuana laced with PCP or formaldehyde—tends to cause more agitation and if used a lot can cause hallucinations and psychosis. Routh was a heavy user. Heavy users become tolerant to the sedation affect. Marijuana goes straight to the brain but settles in the fat all over the body. It causes a contraction of the attention span, and it deadens the senses of the body that are more in touch with the world. You can test positive for marijuana two weeks to thirty days after using. Blood tests can determine how much marijuana is in your body. Reaction context-driven alcohol works differently. It starts in the front of the brain and works its way back. If you keep drinking, it eventually reaches the back of the brain and you pass out. The body eliminates alcohol through the kidneys. In a cannabis high, the euphoria levels off. Pilots who were tested after smoking marijuana slept through the night, and the next morning after psychological tests of the evaluation of coping skills were reviewed, they were still determined to be impaired. Hydro swag, a type of high-quality marijuana, packs a high that lasts up to four to six hours. Eddie would reuse it so he had no hangovers. He was heavily involved in marijuana as testified by his girlfriend, who complained about him smoking marijuana all the time.

Dr. Arambula reiterates that Eddie was offended when doctors with social or medical backgrounds didn't shake his hand. Eddie always wanted to serve in the military and have a four-star hat. He was trained as a gun repairman and guard. He didn't see combat. He went to Iraq to fight but didn't get to experience it. In Haiti, he was aboard ship the whole time, taking care of things coming and going in and out of the ship. He wanted to do more in the military. Eddie had abuse issues in the military with Crown Royal and then vodka in orange juice that he drank in the morning. Eddie met a patient once who sat on his feet and held his ankles down, and this spooked Eddie.

Dr. Arambula continues to tell how Eddie went to work every day and wanted to get paid. On February 1, 2013, he smoked and drank after work. On February 2, 2013, he drank alcohol with coffee, smoked pot, and then left with Chris and Chad. He and Chris had spoken a couple of times before. Eddie told the doctor that he didn't like Chad being there. He got into the backseat and smelled a musky odor. Something was not right, Eddie thought. When they got to the gun range, it was up a hill, and he thought it was fancy. He was suspicious of Chad and Chris but turned his back to them. The doctor says this proves he was not afraid of Chris and Chad or he would not have ever turned his back on people with loaded guns. He told the doctor that when he started shooting Chad, everything was in slow motion. By and large if someone has mental illness, they are reluctant to say so. "I have PTSD"—that is all Eddie said, over and over. The doctor said that the feeling of everything being in slow motion was a sign of marijuana intoxication. Eddie said, "If I had only shot Chad, then Chris would have shot me." So, he shot Chris too.

Dr. Arambula says, "As long as you're intoxicated, the game is over. Even if he has severe mental disease, when he gets drunk, the game is over.

"Immediately after getting out of the truck, Eddie thought something bad was happening. He got out of the truck with his hands up and laid down. This means he knew murder had been his full intent. Eddie was violently intoxicated. He knew it was wrong and he had broken the law. The interview with Ranger Briley, the video of Eddie's backseat trip in the police car, and Eddie's insanity are all a red herring. Eddie was setting up his defense, but the intoxication embellishes the mood swings, which Eddie does have."

To me the testimony of Dr. Arambula brings a lot of sanity to a trial that is questioning whether the defendant is insane. Is he insane or mentally affected by alcohol and drugs and clever enough to fake the insanity? He has certainly had plenty of practice with all the missed jail time by being sent to mental hospitals instead.

The defense gets up slowly and walks toward Dr. Arambula, then stops and says, "You are proud to be on the Texas Medical Board."

The doctor replies, "It is long hours, and it is all for the citizens. Plus, I consult at Three Rivers. What Eddie was doing made a lot of sense in acting out trying to build a defense for himself. Marijuana affects the cerebellum, the back of the brain, the part of the brain that affects coordination and balance."

The defense asks if the association of marijuana use enters into the toxicology report, which takes in heavy metals, pesticide chemicals, and radiation. The doctor replies, "I don't have that degree. How long and how marijuana affects a person depends on the tolerance a person has built up for coordination, balance, and thinking. The kinetics for marijuana are very complicated. Intoxication is more than the euphoria. Everything is not known about marijuana, but since it is legal in Colorado, maybe there will be more studies and we can learn a lot more about marijuana intoxication." Dr. Arambula continues by saying, "I have an opinion, and it just so happens to match with other doctors' opinions." The defense sits down.

The DA gets up and asks, "Why do you not shake hands with prisoners?"

Dr. Arambula says, "Because of masturbation—that is all."

Continuing, the DA says, "Eddie went down range while Chris and Chad were shooting targets. This proves he was not afraid of either one of them. He turned his back on both of them while they were shooting. Eddie was acting normally enough the week of the murder that he didn't miss a day of work."

Judge Cashon decides to quit for the day. He wishes the jury a good weekend and reminds them not to talk to anyone or each other about the trial. They are dismissed, then the victims and defendant families, then the rest of us.

Dr. Arambula walks down the aisle. This man was put on the Texas Medical Board by Governor Rick Perry. He is a short and stocky man who walks, talks, and oozes success. He is a Mexican and like most is very proud of it. I can tell by looking and listening, Dr. Arambula is a hardworking, honest man. He has impressed me greatly. People like Dr. Arambula help make Texas the great state it is.

I give credit to my retail and coaching experiences when I say, "I consider myself a good judge of character." Beginning with many little league softball and baseball seasons that led to championship titles and then reentering and graduating from college in my forties with a BS in education, I then moved on to high school baseball coaching. This resulted in leading a high school team to five state championships by teaching them how to swing the bat, all while keeping the egos of young athletes and their families in check. Yes, sometimes even grandparents feel the need to dole out advice or opinions. The patience that it takes to coach and the ability to read a person's capabilities can be related to understanding what the witnesses are thinking.

It is the weekend, and I have decided not to go home. I am going to spend the weekend in Stephenvillle, Texas, since I am paying for my room by the week. Every day I have been at the courthouse at daybreak to get a place in line, and it is dark or nearly dark every day when court adjourns. Tomorrow will be Saturday and the first day I will have the opportunity to roam around town.

I get up Saturday morning and begin exploring this quaint little city. There are a lot of signs throughout Stephenville in support of Chris Kyle and Chad Littlefield. I am hungry and find a restaurant I have not noticed before. I get out of my car, and guess who I see with what looks to be his family? It is the DA. I didn't expect to see a familiar face and am surprised there is no security around him. Conceal and carry law has its virtues.

Stephenville had a big pecan crop this year, and a lot of pecans are still on the trees. The live oak trees are green and beautiful. North of town is a university-operated milk farm. Stephenville looks a whole lot like Healdton, Oklahoma, the south-central Oklahoma town I grew up in. Stephenville is the home of Tarleton State University, of which Chris Kyle was alumni. The campus sits pretty much right in the middle of Stephenville. Other alumni are George Kennedy, molecular biologist Millie Hughes, who flew aboard NASA space shuttle, Max Diesel, Norman Edward Shunway, father of the heart transplant, and Charles Steen, who discovered uranium in Utah.

I found Stephenville an interesting place. Stephenville, Texas, the Erath County seat, was the number one producer of milk and number one dairy county in Texas in 1972 and had $223,000,000 in milk sales annually. *Moo-la*. I have never been served milk in frosted mugs like beer until I came here. I must say it is the best milk I ever drank. Also in 2004 and 2005, a large number of UFO sightings were reported.

Located on the northeast corner of the courthouse lawn Stephenville displays pride in being the largest milk producer in Texas.

The *Dallas Morning News* has published that interview Tasha Tsiaperas did with me a few days ago. I found it Saturday in the crime section. It is about the trial. I was surprised that I was featured, named, and quoted in the article. Here is the article:

> Days before the capital murder trial of an ex-Marine accused of killing former Navy SEAL Chris Kyle and another man, Robert Blevins got a feeling he needed to head to Texas. The Oklahoma retiree had never watched a trial before, but something about this one was nagging at him. "Something told me, 'You need to go to this trial,'" Blevins said, "I came here to honor a hero. I just wanted to see what took this man's life." Blevins, wearing a dark-colored suit and clutching a yellow legal pad, was one of the first people to line up outside the Erath county courthouse two weeks ago to attend the first day of the trial. But,

dozens of other spectators join him each day, getting up before sunrise to compete with media hordes for about 100 seats in the courtroom. Some, like Blevins, have traveled hundreds of miles for the historic trial. Some are inquisitive townsfolk. Some are Kyle's old friends. But all of them are here to see firsthand what happens to Eddie Ray Routh, the man accused of killing America's deadliest sniper and his best friend, Chad Littlefield, at a shooting range near Glen Rose.[4]

---

[4] Tasha Tsiaperas, "'American Sniper' Trial Draws Daily Regulars," *Dallas Morning News,* February 21, 2015.

Day 9: Monday, February 23, 2015

The ninth day of the trial is Monday, February 23, 2015. I wake earlier than usual to thunder. When I look out the window, I see that we are having a thunder-sleet storm. Yes, it is lightning, thundering, and sleeting very heavily. I start my car to give it plenty time to thaw out and go back inside to dress. I put my suit on and go to the courthouse, park, and wait. I see a police officer finally putting up the barricade to block off the street on the east side of Donald R. Jones Justice Center. I begin keeping an eye on the line of people who will enter the court house. There is no one getting in line. I figure it is due to it being so cold and the sleet. Once I see a half dozen people start getting in line, I will get out of my warm car to join them. I am thinking the trial may not continue today. There is no telling where some of these jurors live and how far they would have to drive in these conditions. I wait and wait a good while, and finally I see the same lady officer pull off the sandbags, lay the barricade down, and pull it off the street. This has to mean a postponement. I get out and check, and sure enough the trial is postponed until 10:00 instead of 9:00. Well, it never happened at 10:00 either. Most of the jury are not able to get here, which is not a surprise because the streets are a solid sheet of ice. Finally, the trial is postponed until Tuesday, February 24, due to weather.

The weather is miserable and roads dangerous. I find a nearby grocery market and buy some golden delicious apples, chocolate milk, regular milk, and a couple of frozen microwave dinners. There's nothing else to do now but go to my room and review my notes and rest until the weather breaks and trial resumes. I take off my suit and lie down in my long handles. Actually, it feels good to take a break. I listen to the news and compare what I hear and see to the reality of the courtroom.

Day 10: Tuesday, February 24, 2015

On Tuesday, February 24, 2015, I arrive early again and see a police officer checking the roof of the justice center. It is two and one half-hours before the trial is to begin. The officer has a rifle with him. It is another very cold morning with lots of ice still on the roads. Today the trial starts an hour and a half late. I am wearing thermal long handles under my suit, a heavy lined tan dress coat with a dark brown fur collar, and rabbit fur–lined leather gloves. The coat and gloves actually came from my department store that I owned twenty years ago. They are both still stylish and quality garments, and I am enjoying the opportunity to wear them. Preparation to venture out this morning has taken longer than usual for everyone, partially because of all the extra clothing necessary to bear the bitter cold. It is also taking extra time for everyone to peel off the layers and to get settled into the courtroom. Needless to say, I am still feeling frozen.

The ninth day of the trial begins with the DA calling Howard J. Ryan to the stand. Eddie Routh is wearing a dark suit, blue shirt, and red tie today. The jury is not yet present. Mr. Ryan is a forensic investigator and tells the court he retired in January 2013 as a lieutenant from the New Jersey state police force following a twenty-five-year career. He has over twenty years of crime scene investigative experience and has conducted over two thousand scene investigations, including hundreds of homicides, death scenes, and shooting investigations. He has testified numerous times as an expert witness in blood stain pattern analyses, crime scene reconstruction investigation, shooting analyses, crime scene processing, and friction ridge processing. He explains that friction ridge processing is film and digital photography, latent print lifts, use of casting material, DNA blood testing, luminal gun residue, metallurgy, ICAL services, and photo lighting. He has also taught in his field of crime scene investigation. He was an instructor in Tennessee and trooper of the year. Ranger Adcock had attended a course taught by Howard J. Ryan and asked if Mr. Ryan could shed some light on the case.

After receiving the autopsy report of both Chris and Chad, crime scene pictures, data of and at the scene, and position of the shooter, Mr. Ryan was able to narrow down the crime scene area. Eddie puts his head up and has stopped his doodling. He is paying attention now to what Mr. Ryan has to say. Mr. Ryan says he is not able to determine the order of the shooting but is able, due to the location of the injuries, to establish multiple shots on the right side.

He says, "You do not see this very often. Normally when one or more shots are fired the victim will move. There was not any movement evident with Chris. Chad was shot in variation of movements by the shooter. Two bullets were shot to Chad's left eye and the top of his head. The body was down lower to the ground. When the bullet went through his face and top of his head, it passed through the body. When a bullet passes through the body, it takes skin, muscle, and hair with it. It seems he was on a knee falling backward as the bullet passed through his head. When a body is against a hard surface, as this body was, and due to the position of the body, the bullet went through the area of the right leg. There was blood accumulation in the thigh and the calf on the right side. There were no entry shots to the right leg area. The front left leg had a transfer pattern with fingers passing through the blood. A contact transfer pattern is very likely. He was shot while on his back. It also shows where the muzzle was located when the shots were fired."

The defense wants to know from Mr. Ryan if this is the first or second shot that was fired. Mr. Ryan replies, "There is no way to know which shot came in what order. There was gunshot residue found, so we know that the gun was at fairly close range, but I am not able to sequence the shots. There is a possibility that two guns were used at once, but not necessarily."

The DA responds, "The gunshots were not point blank, but the shots were not that far away either due to the flight pattern position."

R. Shay Isham, one of the defense attorneys, stands and comments, "Gunshot residue on the body was odd. An odd place, but not on the hand."

Mr. Ryan is asked to leave the stand.

The jury comes in at this time. We all rise, and the trial begins. Taya Kyle is wearing jeans and a sweater and looks very tired. She is a strong woman, but the trial seems to be wearing on her.

The DA calls Howard Ryan back to the stand. Now, by looking at this man I can see that he has experienced a lot. This New Jersey investigator has eyes that look cold. He informs the court that he is a specialist in crime scene reconstruction and liquid blood disposed on bodies and other surfaces, along with blood analyses in flight pattern and blood stain pattern analyses. He states he was an instructor in metro area of Atlanta, Georgia, and at the University of Tennessee National Forensic Academy. He taught Texas Rangers in classes and was asked by one ranger if he could assist in a shooting reconstruction. Mr. Ryan was furnished with crime scene photographs and autopsy reports and had formulated an opinion of the approximate vicinity of the shooter. Blood stain and wound paths keyed into movement confirmed the location of the gunshot wounds.

Mr. Ryan concludes that Chris's wounds were all in one part of the body. He says, "When gunfire erupts, people move. A person knows he or she may be shot at next. Chris never saw it coming. The angle taken showed a photo tight pattern and tight area to achieve that grouping of shots. A wound stain check showed it struck Chris's spinal cord and he was put down right away at a relatively short range. The gunshot residue on the clothes of Chris Kyle was pushed by the gunpowder in the back of the bullet. Some of the gunpowder burns and some does not, but it all comes out of the barrel. The bullet goes far but the residue does not, leaving a presence of residue but not a pattern of residue. There will be a confined pattern of residue two to six feet away. This pattern was not on Chris Kyle. If you shoot a deer at one hundred yards there is no residue pattern. Test fires are upwind and downwind. The wind has an effect on residue patterns.

"The medical examiner described and recorded the shots but not in the order of the shots. Shots numbered five and six on the diagram entered first. One hit the spinal column, causing the victim to fall straight down, where he was found. There was no movement from either of the victims. Both went to the ground where they had been standing. All the blood is right in that place. They did not walk or crawl. The gun was close enough for gun residue saturation underneath the head and bodies. Both received a portion of gunfire standing up, then additional gunshots after falling down. Both individuals were armed and holstered. Mr. Kyle was not facing fire because if he were, he would have reacted. There was a pistol on the ground where shots were fired by Mr. Kyle. They were not long-distance or complicated shots. The shots hit different sides of the body. They could have been shot simultaneously. Chris was shot in the back, with one hit to the spinal cord. He went down immediately. Chad was on a knee or both knees with his head down. That is when he was shot in the head. The blood flowed down his right shoulder and arm. The blood was flowing on the arm and to the leg. The head was bent over when the shot to the head occurred. The blood flowed down the right arm; then he fell backward."

Eddie has his head up and is paying close attention to what is being said. Only he knows exactly how it happened. Chad's mother and father are not here, probably because they do not want to relive the details of their son's murder. Eddie is not taking his eyes off of the screen.

Mr. Ryan continues. "It is showing Chad's body with all the blood surrounding him on the floor of the wooden pavilion at the shooting range. It shows his hand that drug through the blood as he was on his knee before falling backward while dragging the hand through the pool of blood. The shooter had to be out in front of him to shoot the top of the head from the angle of the shot entry. There is some forward splatter showing a front entrance wound."

Eddie now has his head back down and is doodling again.

Mr. Ryan believes the most plausible scenario would be the hand touching the floor and the blood shed on Chad's arm and then onto the floor. He was shot in the face and the back of the head with his left hand on the deck.

The second scenario is that Chad was shot twice in the back and then the shooter came from behind the victim and shot him in the head and below the eye socket. However, Mr. Ryan did not see any residue on Chad's face. It is more plausible that Chad Littlefield was shot in the back and that shot sent him to his knees. The forward splatter to the face ended up in the back because he was against a hard surface and the bullet lost enough energy and stayed there.

This ends the first half of day nine of the trial. When I watched and heard this testimony, and now as I write it, the same thing happens to me. I feel nauseated, hot, and sick.

The second half of today's trial begins, and Marcus Luttrell, author of *Lone Survivor*, his true story of survival and eye witness account of Operation Redwing, and the last hero of the Seal Team 10, is standing in the back of the courtroom. He is a retired US Navy SEAL and shows up to sit with Chris's Kyle's family. He shakes hands with Chris's mom and dad.

Mr. Ryan is still on the stand and says that they found a bullet inside the victim's clothing. Mr. Ryan thought it had been stopped by the composite wood on the deck, as it is hard but still flexible.

The defense attorney, R. Shay Isham, asks Mr. Ryan if this says anything about the defendant, and he replies, "No."

The DA recalls to the stand Captain Upshaw, the head administrator and head of staff at the jail where Eddie Routh was held after the murders. A couple of recorded phone calls to Eddie are played. There are four calls altogether on April 11, 2014, and May 31, 2013. On April 11, 2014, the recorded message says, "Say your name" and we hear from Eddie. "Eddie Routh. Pigs show, black dude that cooks pigs, BBQ joint one hour away at Macedonia, Boss Hog." The recorded message says, "A dollar and twenty-five cents plus fifty cents for every additional minute." Then Eddie again begins talking. "Infinitive network. It is morning in Texas. The sun came up bright on my ass. I read some letters, stuff like that. I mailed it to you. Do your thing about that day in February. I feel shitty about it. I've felt bad about it; wish I hadn't done it. I tried to talk to them. I broke up with Jen that morning. Told her to kick rocks that morning."

This is the conversation on June 3, 2013, between Eddie and Nicholas Schmidle, the reporter for the *New Yorker* and author of, "In the Crosshairs."

"We were headed to the range. I got up early, had a bacon, egg, and cheese sandwich. We stopped at a What-a-burger. I didn't tell them I wasn't hungry. I am tired of eating all that shit day after day. When we got out, Chris was shooting a forty-five. He handed me a forty-five navy pistol. Pretty sure it was a single action. I picked up the nine mm and shot a round. I loaded up again. It smelled like shit that morning. I hauled ass. I stopped at a Dollar General and the line was too fucking long. I said, 'Fuck this' and went to my uncle's house. Both of them were shooting at targets. He was shooting at a fifty-yard target, and I was shooting at a twenty-five-yard target. I asked Chad, 'Why are you not shooting?' Shoot? I didn't shoot Chris first. No, I shot him second. I turned, shot Chad first. Chris just finished a magazine. He was shooting a forty-five. I guess I should pick up a forty-five. It worked better. I couldn't trust them. It smelled like cologne. They were giving me love and hate. I could smell that in the truck. Yeah, I was in the backseat."

Schmidle says, "So you went to your uncle's house." That was the end of this recorded conversation.

Captain Upshaw is excused from the stand, and the defense calls Dr. Dunn, a board-certified psychiatrist. He says, "You heard them siding up against my client, Eddie Routh, on the phone recording of shooting Chris Kyle and Chad Littlefield."

Dr. Dunn replies, "He is schizophrenic and has a mental disorder by disorderly thinking. It is not caused by drugs. He is delusional. He has disorganized speech, social withdrawal, and bipolar disorder. His medical record at the VA is evidence that supports a mood disorder. My diagnosis is schizophrenia. He was dismissed with a mood disorder. It is a common claim on the records. Largely, depressed people are warranted to have delusional thinking. At the hospital, I work at, one of these types of patients believes he is president of the United States. You don't take into account the number of delusional patients.

"Eddie's belief that a member of the Mexican Mafia is living next door to him was delusional thinking. Mr. Routh's thoughts were moving around. Dr. Arambula's testimony that if you are intoxicated, the game is over. It is not over because someone was intoxicated. The prosecution's theory is a red herring. Eddie is mentally ill instead of sane enough to realize what he did was wrong."

Mr. Dunn is trying to make the case for the defendant Eddie Routh by laying doubt in the jury's mind. He tells the court, "When Eddie talks, he doesn't make a lot of sense. He has real problems. In hospitals, two-thirds of people in mental institutions have schizophrenia. We don't have any patients who are induced by drugs. He was a paranoid and schizophrenic patient. Eddie knows he is paranoid. He was told he was delusional. He thought Chris and Chad were going to take him out. The prosecution said Eddie was jealous of Chris. Nothing in my records shows that had anything to do with the shooting. Eddie thought he was going to die."

This guy, Dr. Dunn, is hard to understand and talks so fast that Mr. Johnson, the stenographer, has to slow him down. He is having trouble keeping up with recording what he has said, and I am having trouble listening to him.

Dr. Dunn states, "Cannabis-induced psychosis is rare." He brings up Eddie's medical records and states that every time he was dismissed from mental institutions, Eddie was treated for mood disorder and psychosis and had different medications for each diagnosis.

I have been keeping an eye on the jury during the entire trial and have not noticed a lot of reaction. But after Dr. Dunn's last testimony, their facial expressions and the eye contact with each other makes me think they don't believe a word Dr. Dunn has said. The judge calls for a break at this time, and the jury is excused. They walk out single file. One jury member is smiling, almost laughing, as he walked out of the courtroom. Only those of us sitting on the far right side of the court could have seen this.

The jury seating in the courtroom.

It is 3:00 p.m., and the break is over. Chad's mother and father show up for the second half. This has been a long day already, and a lot of information has been given.

Mr. Dunn is still on the stand, and the DA is speaking. "On January 19, Eddie was a user of marijuana. Do you have to let a patient dry out before you can make a proper diagnosis?" The doctor agrees. The DA says that Eddie was admitted for threatening homicide, calling his girlfriend a crack whore, and he was not interrogated in a criminal way as if he had carried out a crime or even been intoxicated. Substance high goes away. Cannabis high goes away. Was he sober? Had the psychosis gone away? You can be mad at someone even if you're mentally ill. On February 2, he lied about smoking pot. He lied about going to the shooting range. Facing capital murder, suspects have thoughts that are inaccurate. Historians call that plain old lies. He had been watching *Boss Hog*, all about pigs, *Seinfeld*, and *The Twilight Zone*. They were all about pig people. "He didn't talk about pigs to the *New Yorker* writer," says the DA. "The VA records on January 30 are that Eddie's marijuana usage was twice daily. It was revised for psychosis that he smoked and drank. He threatened a nurse on the doctor's visit when he was admitted for pulling a knife. He was a different person at that time."

The defense attorney, Saint-John, stands up and attempts to strongly emphasize that the defendant is insane. He says "Every time I see a Chris, I am sent to another Chris, victim after victim. On February 2, 2013, I believe Eddie Routh was psychotic."

This defense is running out of time to persuade the jury that their client is truly insane. I am thinking that last defensive comment from Saint-John can be considered null, ineffective, and useless. The atmosphere in the courtroom is unnerving. The tension is building, and closing arguments are looming.

The DA rises and confidently accesses the facts. He affirms, "Eddie loaded a nine mm before he left the crime scene. Then went home to get his dog. Then he was surrounded by police and fled on a high-speed chase. He told the doctor he did it. Eddie said, 'I made a mistake.' You have got to believe him. He was telling the truth when he said, 'They were going to kill me, so I had to kill them.'"

We take a break, and on the video screen in the courtroom are bold letters, visible, and left out for all to see.

**State of Texas
vs.
Eddie Ray Routh
Capital Murder**

I start to leave the courtroom during the break but notice the DA roaming around, and I see him approach Chris Kyle's father. They spend a few minutes talking. I also see Jane Starnes, assistant from the office of the Texas attorney general, having words with Chad Littlefield's mother. What I would give to feel free to join them in conversation. After being here for nearly two weeks, in my mind, I have begun to feel like a piece of everything that has gone on.

Closing Arguments

Jane Starnes rises slowly and walks toward the jury but pauses as if to emphasize the weight of the words she is about put upon them. She begins the closing arguments by telling the jury, "You know more about this trial than anyone else. It is unfair to call this trial 'The American Sniper Trial.' There were two people killed." She begins to pace and further says, "Chad Littlefield was a father, a brother, and a son. He did not have a movie or a book." She is now looking at the jury eye-to-eye, saying, "Chris and Chad were friends, outdoorsmen. They thought what they were doing was therapeutic. They overrode the feelings they had about Eddie and let his fruit flag fly. We don't know why they said he was straight up nuts."

Ms. Starnes resumes pacing while talking to the jury. "They got all those guns out to shoot and put a loaded gun in Eddie Routh's hand. In the last two weeks, we have given Eddie Routh a fair trial. You listened to nine days of evidence. You heard, saw, and followed the law. The burden of proof beyond a shadow of doubt happened in Erath County. He got out of the truck with his hands up intentionally and knowing, not premeditated, that he shot Chris six times and Chad seven times deliberately and calculated. He waited until Chris's gun had spent its shells before firing. He shot Chad in the back and then shot Chris in the back. Chris, who survived four tours in Iraq, died face down in the dirt after being shot in the back. Chad saw one of those bullets coming, and Eddie finished him off. He wanted Chad dead, dead, dead, dead when he left the crime scene. Eddie Routh knew Chris would kill him, so he had to kill Chris. Fifteen bullets in a 9-mm sig. Why did he reload it and get away from the bloody mess? He went to his sister's house, went to Taco Bell. Chad's DNA was on the defendant's boots. When Eddie was standing over Chad's head and shooting him, he got blood on his boot. This proved that he did this crime. A senseless crime. We don't have to prove he is sane. The defense has to prove he is insane—the definition of all three parts of insanity."

Ms. Starnes continues, saying, "Eddie Routh used a lot of marijuana. The charge is voluntary intoxication. The bottom line is he knows what he did was wrong. He sets up this pattern when he gets into trouble. He says he is nuts and ends up in the hospital. He thought he would pull this off again. People lie to get out of trouble. They don't lie to get into trouble. The whole family smoked marijuana. What was in that bong that Ranger Briley found? Was it marijuana laced with chemicals? He smoked two bowls and drank whiskey that morning. He experienced paranoia after smoking. He stayed high for four to five hours and was under the influence when he killed those men. Reference the Texas Penal Code 801 about insanity. Dr. Arambula said Routh's actions speak louder than words. He went down range while they were shooting, demonstrating that he was not afraid of the victims. He shot them out of anger. It is incredible that you can kill two men and then go to Taco Bell, acting well enough to make an order and pick it up. Then during a standoff with Lancaster police, he participated in a high-speed chase of over one hundred miles per hour through red lights and stop signs. Eddie Routh knew what he had done was wrong. First he said, 'They wouldn't talk to me.' They got killed by this guy because they wouldn't talk to him! He was running to Oklahoma to get away. 'They were going to barbeque my ass.'

"Ranger Briley asked him, 'What did you do after you shot them?' He replied, 'I fled. I would like to see my mom one last time.' He was asked, 'What would you tell the family?' The answer was, 'I'm sorry.' He told Dr. Dunn, 'Pretty shitty thing to do, to kill someone' and 'I figured I would get arrested soon. I did it. I knew I made a mistake. Running from the police was dumb.' Eddie was mad about What-a-burger, mad about them not shaking his hand, mad they didn't talk to him. He did not want to shoot them in the truck because he was afraid he would get hurt. Dr. Price was told by Eddie, 'I shot the target but was so bothered by Chad. Why shoot Chris? Because he would have killed me.'"

The defense attorney, Tim Moore, rises and waits a few minutes before speaking to the jury. "You have to decide why Eddie Routh shot two men he had never met in his life. He didn't know what he was doing. It was wrong, that is pretty obvious. He shot these two men. You have to judge the facts. The law and evidence cannot do this."

Mr. Moore is attempting to get the attention of one of the jurors. I can't really see what is going on, but I think he is referring to a juror whom he caught napping or who seemed not to be paying attention. Out of the blue he makes this off-the-wall statement: "What would I say to a neighbor or people at church if she slept, but with one eye open? I have been saturated in this trial."

Mr. Moore continues with closing arguments. "The chemist said it was just plain marijuana. It was the defendant's right to testify or not to testify."

"There are two important things about being guilty of capital murder and not guilty by reason of insanity. Eight of you might be one way and four of you the other way. Don't violate your conscience by switching just to go along with the crowd. At the time of the charges, the defendant did not know that his conduct was wrong. Wrong is not defined. We know we have the burden to prove he was insane at the time of the murder.

"Automatic punishment of life in prison without the possibility of parole? Look at the time lapse from when Eddie smoked that bowl or two of marijuana. The effects might last two to four hours. The murders had to have happened around four o'clock in the afternoon. The marijuana would have worn off. Eddie was taken by Ranger

Briley at eleven p.m. At the time Eddie was talking gibberish. The judge was at the scene and signed the search warrant. Every bit of evidence was collected—enough for probable cause. A blood sample was taken from Eddie. He was insane when he shot those two people. He had even gone to the VA and Green Oaks Hospitals several times for treatment for mental disorders. Dr. Dunn works with psychotic patients every day. It is a textbook case that Eddie was insane at the time of the shootings."

Defense Attorney Isham takes over and states, "Absolutely the video does not have a dog in the fight. Eddie Ray Routh negotiated an order at Taco Bell in Red Oak, Texas. Any single fact can be looked at two or three different ways. You did see the police there when Eddie went to pick up his dog."

Before resuming his closing argument, Isham keeps rubbing his face and scratching his head as if he is beyond frustration. He carries on, saying, "Actions, words, and opinions with some going a while back—some three weeks ago. We rolled through this trial in a limited amount of time. We have got a veteran, a marine, who has problems!

"In 2011 the VA told Eddie, 'You do not have a tapeworm.' Eddie showed signs of schizophrenia. He had delusions of having a tapeworm. It is abundantly clear that Eddie smoked marijuana. Everyone who knew Eddie said it calmed him down. There is evidence that he didn't handle his alcohol well. Dr. Dunn said Eddie has the symptoms of schizophrenia. Eddie thought he was going to be killed, and other times he thought he was going to die. He smelled things in the air, which is another example of delusions. It paints a picture of Eddie suffering from schizophrenia. He has nothing to gain by making things up.

"When Jennifer Weed lived with Eddie, she describes him staring at walls and laughing and sweating through his shirt. There were periods when he was not violent but paranoid; looking outside windows and not wanting to go outside. He didn't want Jennifer Weed to talk at the house because 'they' could hear what goes on. The hospital was giving him antipsychotic medication; he is riding a roller coaster of emotions. The assumption was made that he smoked marijuana when getting up at four thirty that morning. When the uncle came over, he talked about spiritual things. He was not intoxicated at four p.m.

"That afternoon there was no evidence that Chris or Chad would have taken someone who smelled of alcohol to the gun range. If he did not know what he was doing, why ask him the questions? Formaldehyde won't keep. It evaporates. Why were there two vials of clear liquid in Eddie's stash that came from the lab? The prosecution admitted they got in there by mistake. Chris said he was 'straight up nuts.' He knew it without knowing how many times he had been in the hospital.

"When Eddie's mother was on the stand, she was asked why she did not warn Chris that Eddie was crazy. The jury cannot be asked to find Eddie Ray Routh not crazy."

Defense Attorney Saint-John rises and puts a picture of Eddie in his uniform with his mother on the screen. "You determine what the truth is. How in the world was Eddie intoxicated at four that afternoon?

"That is Eddie." Saint-John points to Eddie in the picture. "He killed those men because he had a delusion. It is all speculation. He took their lives because he thought they were going to kill him. The state of Texas wants you to believe Eddie killed them because they didn't shake his hand and so forth. Look at the delusion in Eddie's mind. The ranger can't change what is in Eddie's mind.

"He told his sister, 'I had to kill two men today. I had to get out of that situation. I was going to be the next one to get his head shot off.' Why would you prescribe antipsychotic medication to someone who was not psychotic? He did commit murder, but at the time of the crime, he did not know what he was doing was wrong. If you are steadfast in what you believe in, do not be persuaded.

"Mrs. Taylor, the woman Eddie worked for at the cabinet shop, was asked, 'Did he go outside to smoke pot at work?' She replied,

'Not that I know of.' DA Nash discovered the vials in the stash box and brought it up to the tech at the lab. He said he made a mistake. He put them in the box by mistake. It was a tragic situation for all of the families."

Attorney Saint-John is throwing out allegations, hoping to put strong enough doubt in just one juror's mind to affect the verdict.

District Attorney Alan Nash is confident and somewhat aggressive when he rises for the final closing argument. He steps in front of his table and stands tall as he looks directly into the jurors' eyes. He is carrying the weight of justice for the American Sniper, an American hero, and his comrade, Chad Littlefield, in the words he is about to present.

He begins, "We have heard for two weeks about violent behavior—the shooting in the back of the head and face. The defense wants him to get away with this performance. Eddie is cool and calm when he is by himself on the video, but when Eddie gets around an audience it is, 'I'm sick, I have PTSD.' He applied for disability and listed ailments of every part of his body in 2012. 'I was in the military. I have PTSD.' What happens? He goes to the hospital. Police show up, it's, 'I'm military. I have PTSD.' In January of 2013, he sobers up. The day he gets out of the hospital, what does he do? He goes and gets high. Every time he showed up at the hospital, he tested positive for cannabis. He is a doper, a hardcore cannabis user. One million men serve in the military. I am tired of people not taking responsibility for what they do. Next step; he just murdered two men in cold blood. When talking to a reporter from New York, he was articulate. He is very clear speaking when it is something he needs. I learned a lot about the defendant. He will shoot people in the back, and then knows how to act when he needs to get out of trouble. He is not one bit sorry for what he did."

District Attorney Nash walks even closer to the jurors, never losing eye contact. He is making eye contact with each and every one of them. His voice gets louder, and he seems angry as he continues to make his closing arguments. "When Justin found the scene, he told the kids to get out of there. He started working on trying to save their lives. Eddie had stood over the victim and shot him in the head and then reloaded the gun. What if Justin had shown up with the kids earlier? What would Eddie have done? We don't know what this defendant is capable of doing."

There may be many in the audience who want to see Eddie Routh get an insanity verdict, but Alan Nash is not one of them. He is pushing hard for a guilty verdict. He looks back and forth at the jury and then at Eddie as he explains why this defendant is guilty of capital murder. He wants this guy in prison for the rest of his life.

Nash sweeps his arm across the jury box and points at the defendant, "What if those officers would have had their backs to him? What would he have done? We have been hearing excuses. The same man who has delusions comes out with his hands up. This is the same man, knowing he killed those two men. Two weeks of excuses! The evidence this defendant left proves that actions speak louder than his words. The words have no meaning; they change to suit whatever he needs."

Someone's phone pings in the courtroom, and Nash slouches at the interruption and looks around to see a woman being escorted out of the courtroom by two officers. Later I was told that is was one of the defense attorney's wife. Absolutely none of us spectators are allowed to bring phones or equipment into the courtroom.

DA Nash continues speaking. "Gasping for life, Chad was shot in the head. It was not enough to incapacitate him; he wanted him dead, *dead, dead*! Find him guilty."

Right after the lady with the phone is escorted out, the prosecution is talking about how Eddie's mother could have warned Chris and Chad about Eddie's condition and things that had happened. Taya Kyle suddenly stands and storms down the aisles past spectators in the courtroom and hits the door hard on her way out. I think she and others believe if Chris had been aware of the entire situation concerning Eddie threatening to kill himself and his violent episodes with his family and girlfriend, this murder would not have happened.

Judge Cashon dismisses the jury to deliberate on their verdict. Justice and Eddie Routh's fate is now in the jury's hands.

In the lobby, there is a lot of speculation on as to how long it will take before the verdict is in. I am wondering if I might be spending the night again.

The Verdict

I am with my two new friends, Vicky, a working veterinarian's wife, and Jim Walton. Jim served our country in Vietnam during 1966 and 1967. In the latter days of the trial, we helped each other by saving places in line. In the beginning, we were all on our own. No one was saving anyone a spot. We decide to go eat at a place one block away. We finish and talk about going back to the Donald R. Jones Justice Center or calling it a night. We go back to the justice center, and I am glad we did. It is around 8:30 or 9:00 p.m., and as we go into the lobby of the court, we hear the verdict is in. This is exciting. We are all nervous to an extent. What if the jury has found him to be guilty by reason of insanity?

Inside DA Nash hugs Chad's mother. Everyone is just kind of milling around. There are a lot of nervous smiles in the crowd. We go sit in our seats and wait. Marcus Luttrell is still here. He is sitting over by Taya's father. I count twenty officers, some in uniform and some in plain clothes. Another six all in plain clothes are up by the judge. The judge and jury have not come in yet. Some newsperson, a young lady, gets escorted out for some reason that I don't know. Both Eddie's parents and Chris's parents are holding each other. Chris's brother is also holding his parents and is looking anxious. You know their stomachs have to be tied up in knots.

The judge scans the courtroom with his eyes before asking the jurors to enter. The jurors walk in single file and take the same seats they have sat in throughout the trial. The courtroom is very quiet, and anticipation can be felt coming from all over the room. A piece of paper is handed to the bailiff. The bailiff hands the verdict to the judge.

Judge Cashon reads the verdict. "Guilty and guilty."

The judge asks each and every jury member if this is their verdict. All twelve reply, "Yes." The judge says, "Then I will enter judgement." Judge Cashon immediately sentences Eddie Routh to life in prison without possibility of parole. "Be careful of what you say," the judge tells the individual members of the jury, "because it is out there forever."

I am trying to absorb everything in the room right now. I look around, trying to see everyone's reaction. There is no emotion from Eddie's mother and father. They have only blank stares on their faces.

On the other side of the room, the victims' families are sighing with relief and smiling at each other. Justice was served; closure can begin. As part of this closure, at this time the court offers the families the opportunity to express to Eddie Routh the effect his actions have had on their lives.

The victim impact statements come from Chad's brother first. He tells Eddie Routh the now-convicted murderer, "Because of you, we have lost a great son, brother, and father. We will forever carry a scar for life. You have destroyed the opportunity to be a real man. Your claims of having PTSD have shamed all veterans who really have it."

Chad's father is next. He says, "Chad was trying to help you. He was a good listener. He tried to give you help. Texas has spared your life, something you did not do for Chad." And because Eddie had said he didn't know Chad's name, Mr. Littlefield says, "For the rest of your life, be reminded of his name." He spells it out loud and clear: *"C H A D L I T T L E F I E L D."* Then he says, *"Chad Littlefield."*

There is a lot of crying and hugging right after the victims' impact statements. Emotions had built up, and the anticipation of waiting for the verdict was overwhelming. The verdict is relief for the Littlefields and Kyles, but still there is nothing to celebrate. Nothing is going to replace their loss.

My new friend Jim Walton shakes Chris's father's hand. I am still sitting right behind Chris's mom and dad. I don't do anything, but I continue to write. I want to hug Mr. Kyle, but I just write and watch.

I follow the families outside. There are twelve cameras with lights and several microphones rigged all together. The lights are bright and blinding. I notice one that says Fox News 10. They are hoping to get a statement from Taya Kyle, but she isn't around anywhere that I can see.

Chad's mother steps up to the microphones and says, "We waited two years for justice for our son. We are thrilled to have the verdict that we have." And referring to the news people, she says, "Thank you for the way you have treated us."

I get up the next morning and make my way back to I-35 northbound to drive home to Oklahoma. When I get there, my son Will and grandson Will and granddaughter Lilly say they saw me on TV news during the trial. They ask, "What are you going to do now, Pa?"

I tell them, "I think I am going to write a book about an American hero."

To all veterans out there who may be reading this book deployed somewhere in a foreign country or rebuilding your life at home, I think I can speak for many and say we are thinking of you, we love you, and we are damn proud of you.

I plan on giving 10 percent of the proceeds of this work to churches and 10 percent to veterans, specifically to Taya Kyle's veteran organization.

The jury room where Eddie Routh was found guilty.

Characters of the Trial

Ronald R. Jones Justice Center—Location of trial.

Thomas D. Johnson—Court stenographer who stopped the trial to slow down Dr. Dunn's speech.

Leanne Littlefield—Chad Littlefield's wife and assistant principal at Midlothian, Texas.

Morgan Littlefield—Chad Littlefield's daughter.

Raymond Routh—Eddie Ray Routh's father.

Jodi Routh—Eddie Ray Routh's mother.

Eddie Ray Routh—Marine corporal and defendant.

Justin Largo—Worked at Rough Creek Lodge.

Ranger Danny Briley—Prosecution witness; crime scene investigator and reenactment; interrogated Eddie Routh.

Tim Moore—Lead defense attorney.

R. Shay Isham—Defense attorney.

Ranger Michael Adcock—Called by defense to identify guns from crime scene.

Jeff Schaffer—Secret Service expert in computer and phone forensics.

Jane Starnes—From the office of Texas attorney general and dead ringer for actress Kathy Bates.

Alan Nash—District attorney.

Judge Jason Cashon—Resided over the trial.

Frank Alvarez—Manager of Rough Creek Lodge.

Chris Scott Kyle—Six foot two, 230 pounds, American sniper, and murder victim of Eddie Ray Routh.

Chad Houston Littlefield—Age thirty-five and murder victim of Eddie Ray Routh.

Judy Littlefield—Chad Littlefield's mother.

J. Warren St. John—Defense attorney.

Ranger Danny Delgado—Witness.

Dr. Randal Price—Psychologist who became DA Nash's best witness; disagreed with Dr. Dunn about Eddie Routh's mental health.

Michael Arambula, MD—First Hispanic president of the Texas Medical Board; appointed by Governor Rick Perry; forensic psychiatry; doctor of pharmacy from the University of Texas; gave quote "Intoxication, game is over."

James Watson—Eddie's uncle and Jodi Routh's brother.

Laura Blevins—Eddie Routh's sister.

Nicholas Schmidle—Reporter from *New Yorker Magazine*; had conversation with Eddie in jail; wrote article titled "In the Crosshairs."

David—EMT who arrived at the murder scene at Rough Creek Lodge and helped work to revive the victims.

Bobby—Off-duty former eight-year fire department lieutenant; heard the call about 5:10, 17:30, 17:40. The second first responder who worked on the victims.

Matt Green—Ambulance driver and third responder to work on the victims.

Office Martin—Deputy of Seminole County; graduated from Police Academy of Texas.

Vanessa Kelly—Was in Oklahoma City at a twirling contest and called Leanne Littlefield on the day of the murder.

Ranger Matt—Arrived at the murder scene at 10:00 p.m. and took 360-degree pictures of the scene; found casing by Chris Kyle's right ear and a 9-mm casing near Chad Littlefield's arm.

Patrol Office Salazar—From Lancaster, Texas; filmed high-speed chase from dash cam and chest cam.

Officer Mike Logan—Friend and neighbor of Eddie Routh.

Officer Grimes—Rammed the truck Eddie was driving.

Ranger David Armstrong—Took pictures at I-35 and searched Eddie Routh's home at 220 West Sixth Street; cross-examined by defense.

Ranger Jim Holland—Carried an ivory-handled pistol.

Sergeant Stewart—Stored evidence gathered.

James Jeffress—Department of Public Safety forensic scientist specializing in ballistics.

Officer Phillips—Sergeant for thirteen years and detox expert.

Captain Upshaw—Instructed Sergeant Phillips to take clothing from Eddie Routh to be processed for evidence; head of administration and staff at the jail; recorded phone calls to and from Eddie Routh.

Ranger Ron Pettigrew—Seven-year Texas Highway Patrolman; five years as a Texas Ranger; met with Laura Blevins and was responsible for securing Chris Kyle's truck to the Garland, Texas lab; found two phones, one belonging to Chris Kyle, and a wallet in the console.

Ranger Mike Gunter—Witness.

Jay Novacek—Tight end for Dallas Cowboys, five-time Pro Bowler, number 84 with three Super Bowl wins; attended the trial.

Amber Moss—ABAS DNA forensic scientist; worked at Texas department crime lab in Garland, Texas; responded to questions from Assistant Attorney General Jane Starnes during capital murder trial.

Donna Taylor—Friend of Eddie Routh's mother and owner of the cabinet shop where Eddie Routh worked; said, "he just seemed bothered."

Jennifer Weed—Friend and girlfriend of Eddie Routh; thought he smoked too much marijuana; was proposed to the night before the murders after a big argument between her and Eddie.

Greg Pruitt—Locked up evidence from Rough Creek Lodge.

James Blevins—Laura Blevins's husband and Eddie Routh's brother-in-law.

Major Dr. Charles Overstreet—Witness called by the defense who was not allowed to testify.

Dr. Mitchell H. Dunn—Doctor who testified for the defense and the prosecution; Dallas MD School Board Certified Psychiatry.

Marcus Luttrell—Navy SEAL present at trial; wrote his story that was made into the movie *Lone Survivor*.

Dr. Davis—Testified he believed Eddie Routh to be insane.

Lt. Michael Smith—Lancaster police officer said, "Routh told us he had taken a couple of souls and had a few more to take."

Howard J. Ryan—Retired lieutenant from New Jersey; instructor who taught crime scene classes in Tennessee.

Tarleton State University—Chris Kyle attended.

Midlothian, Texas—Where Eddie Routh went to school.

Lake Oswego—Place where Taya Kyle was born.

frog skeleton—Symbol for fallen Navy SEAL; Chris Kyle's tattoo.

DHL license—Streamline shipping process to eliminating extra steps with online shipping; helps to get set up to ship ITAR Commodities (a.k.a. International Traffic and Arms Regulations).

PTSD—Post-traumatic stress disorder.

9 mm Sig Sauer Pistol—Weapon found in door of Chris Kyle's truck and gun that killed Chad Littlefield.

glass vials—Presented earlier as belonging to Eddie Routh. DA Allen Nash's unartful questioning likely made jurors believe the vials stored in evidence boxes containing drug paraphernalia seized from Routh's house belonged to him. Testimony shows that crime lab workers had put vials in the evidence boxes to preserve drug evidence. Vials were disallowed as evidence.

Definitions

antipsychotic medication—A class of psychiatric medication primarily used to manage psychosis, particularly in schizophrenia and bipolar disorder.[1]

forensic psychology—The intersection between psychology and the justice system. Professional practice by psychologist within an area of clinical psychology, counseling psychology, school psychology, or another specialty recognized by the American Psychological Association when engaged as experts and represent themselves as such. [2]

mental illness—Mayo Clinic refers to wide range of mental health conditions and disorders that affect your mood thinking and behavior. Examples of mental illness include depression, anxiety disorder, schizophrenia, eating disorder, and addictive behavior.[3]

paranoia—A thought process believed to be highly influenced by anxiety or fear. Involves feelings of perception and exaggerated sense of importance.[4]

psychiatry—Medical specialty devoted to the study, diagnosis, treatment, and prevention of mental disorders. Wikipedia[5]

psychologist—Evaluates and studies behavior and mental process.[6]

psychology—Study of mind and behavior. An academic discipline and applied science that seeks to understand individuals and groups by establishing general principles and researching specific cases. [7]

psychosis—Also called psychotic disorder. A mental disorder characterized by a disconnection from reality.[8]

schizophrenia—A brain disorder in which people interpret reality abnormally.[9]

---

1   http://www.webmd.com/mental-health/medications-treat-disorders
2   https://www.bing.com/search?q=forensic+psychology&form=EDGEAR&qs=MB&cvid=6858fa1260594954aafac6f1f30490fd&pq=forensic+psychology&elv=AM6mMsAKJ3dH5JctdgPPZ5Bnve79aFektV9jzeyF8S8M
3   http://www.mayoclinic.org/diseases-conditions/mental-illness/basics/definition/CON-20033813
4   https://en.wikipedia.org/wiki/Para
5   https://en.wikipedia.org/wiki/Psychiatry
6   https://en.wikipedia.org/wiki/Psychologist
7   https://en.wikipedia.org/wiki/Psychology
8   https://en.wikipedia.org/wiki/Psychosis
9   http://www.mayoclinic.org/diseases-conditions/schizophrenia/home/ovc-20253194

I want to thank, Carol, my wife of forty-four years, for her time and patience with helping me and typing this book.

Robert F. Blevins

About the Author

Robert Blevins was born in Carter County Oklahoma and raised in the small town of Healdton living there for 49 years. He was third generation owner/manager of Massad's Department Store. He and his wife have 2 daughters, 2 sons and 8 grandchildren. At age 45, Robert acquired a BS from Southeastern Oklahoma State University in Durant, Oklahoma.

Raising cattle, farming and training hunting dogs are a few of his talents. Coaching his children and grandson little league softball and baseball earned many championships. He later assisted coaching his son's high school baseball team to five state championships. After surviving colon cancer Robert retired. He is now known locally as Master Gardener, and can be found peddling his crops at local farmer's markets near Yukon, Oklahoma.

Printed in Great Britain
by Amazon